YouTube Blueprint For Beginners

The Strategies & Secrets To Starting & Rapidly Growing Your Channel, Becoming A Video Influencer, Mastering Social Media Marketing, Advertising & SEO

Brandon's Business guides

Table of Contents

Introduction

Do you want to become the next YouTube sensation but don't know where to start? Or maybe you want to use YouTube to grow your business but don't know exactly what your options are? Even if you just want to share your views on various topics with other people, but don't know where to start, this book will help you. Whether you already have a YouTube channel that you're planning to grow, or you just want to start one, this book will provide you with the essential information that you need to succeed.

Some people find it difficult to get started because they lack ideas or knowledge. Others don't really understand how YouTube actually works. It is time to stop overthinking, and start doing. YouTube is a user-friendly social media platform, but it is understandable if you have some fears that can only be dispersed by the certainty that comes with knowledge. The tips and techniques included in this book will help you not only to get started, but to also develop your channel, gather subscribers, and become a YouTube star!

It might feel odd reading a book on YouTube when you can just watch a few YouTube videos about YouTube. There is loads of information on YouTube about YouTube itself. However, you already know you should not trust everything you see or read on the internet. I spent years researching, developing, and growing together with the YouTube platform. By following all the changes that YouTube went through, and learning how to adapt to the numerous updates, I gathered enough expertise to help work with other channels as their producer and adviser. And even though you can find various videos on YouTube on how to build your subscriber base, or how to produce a good video, get awesome ideas, you would have to spend hundreds of hours searching for quality material. This book gathers all that information in one place, allowing you to come back to it and easily find everything you need at any given moment.

Learn about the rich but brief history of YouTube, or what equipment you should invest in. See the changes the platform went through, how it developed from a place where people shared their videos, to a full-blown social media platform. Did you know YouTube is the second biggest search engine in the world? Right after Google! Billions of people browse through various videos each hour of the day. People use it to find entertainment, to listen to relaxing music while they work, or to learn new skills or acquire new knowledge. Even academics use YouTube platforms to upload their lectures and share them with students all around the world. The possibilities are endless and if you know how to take advantage of them, you will succeed.

Learn how to start your own channel, how to develop your art, produce your first video and find your own niche in which you will leave a part for yourself. Connect with other Youtubers and with the audience by learning how to properly use other social media platforms to drive traffic to your channel. In order to be found, you will also need to learn the tricks of the trade, such as SEO and the importance of keywords. YouTube is special when it comes to SEO because it relies more on community engagement than on backlinks and website crawling. Optimize your YouTube channel in order to attract the right type of audience, and in order to let the internet know what your videos are about. Only this way you will ensure the visibility and reach of your videos.

Learn about recording your videos, how to compose the scenes, what background to use, and how it all comes down to the niche you are working in. Learn how to edit your videos and get them up on YouTube. Do you still lack ideas for your first video? Or maybe you are already famous and you feel like you exhausted all your inspiration? In this book, you will find a list of things you could do next and find that elusive inspiration instead of waiting for it to come to you.

If you own a business and you want to learn how to use YouTube as a marketing tool, there is something for you in this book too. Since YouTube is part of social network marketing, you will learn all about how advertising works, how to drive traffic to your business' website, how to brand your YouTube channel or promote your already existing brand. And finally, you'll learn how you can use other YouTubers who cater to wide audiences, as the face behind your brand, as promoters and influencers who can convince their audience to buy your product or service.

Finally, if you are a YouTuber who wants to start earning a living from his content, you'll learn how to properly monetize your channel. Whether through ads, by becoming an influencer, or by setting up your own merchandising store.

Television programming is history. YouTube is the place to be. Whether you just want to stand in front of the audience and show them what you got, want to grow your business, earn money through YouTube, or become a famous gamer, you should grasp the opportunity and join the millions of content creators already on YouTube.

You might have heard that the time of YouTube stars is passing and that it is impossible to become famous these days, but that's not true. Yes, the competition is fiercer than ever, and you need to be unique in some way to stand out in the sea of content creators, but it is still possible as long as you play your cards right. In some ways, it's actually easier nowadays to make it on YouTube than a decade ago. So, start today because the opportunity is right in front of you, all you need to do is seize it!

Section 1:

Exploring YouTube

Chapter 1 - How Much Do You Know About YouTube?

Nowadays, YouTube is a part of everyday life and everyone knows what it is. It's a household name. It's hard to imagine that not that long ago we didn't have a massive online video platform where we could look up everything from funny cat videos to programming tutorials. During the dark ages of the 2000s, people used dial-up to connect to the Internet, and sharing videos was always a struggle. YouTube was revolutionary.

YouTube is a massive entertainment and advertising platform and a search engine in its own right, trailing behind only Google. But until 2005, nobody knew what they were missing. The platform started like most websites and online platforms: as an unknown startup somewhere in Silicon Valley.

YouTube, an Ongoing History of Videos and Comments

YouTube's humble beginnings can be traced back to February 2005 when three former PayPal employees, Chad Hurley, Steve Chen, and Jawed Karim, envisioned a new idea. That's when they registered the youtube.com domain. Their objective was to create an online video-sharing platform where users could upload their videos for others to watch. At that time, YouTube was a dream, Facebook didn't exist, and everyone relied on messenger apps for communication. But things were about to change faster than anyone could anticipate.

YouTube was up and running, but videos couldn't be uploaded to the platform until April 23rd. That's the day when Chad Hurley posted the first video in YouTube's history, and it was a short 18 seconds long clip of him visiting the zoo in San Diego. The video wasn't anything spectacular, but it marked the beginning of the Internet as we know it today.

Initially, the founders intended to allow users to share videos with their friends and family. The videos weren't supposed to be public. As a result, there were only 19 videos uploaded to

YouTube during the first two months of its launch and they had gathered an insignificant number of views. That was all about to change when the 20th video was uploaded.

In May 2005, YouTube became accessible to a limited number of beta users. The platform started growing, hosting more videos with each passing day, and on June 26th the first viral video was uploaded. Two kids dubbing a song by the Backstreet Boys made history by recording themselves and uploading their video titled "Tow chinese boys: i want it that way". Their hit also made history by becoming one of YouTube's first videos with a typo in the title. By 2021 the video gathered around 7 million views, which doesn't sound like much for a viral video by today's standards. But back then social media was in its infancy and even a few thousand views was something big.

The website's official launch date was December 15, 2005, and by that time it was already registering roughly two million views per day. That number started growing exponentially as YouTube reached 25 million views in the next two months. By July, the platform reached a major milestone, registering 100 million daily views with over 60,000 videos being uploaded each day. However, rapid growth came with a new set of challenges for the founders.

As traffic demands increased, the company had to regularly upgrade its hardware. New equipment was purchased to keep up with the high influx of new users and the sheer number of videos that were being hosted. Nonetheless, upgrading computers and investing in more broadband connections wasn't the biggest concern. YouTube started attracting the eyes of the media and entertainment industry. Some of the videos the users were uploading contained copyrighted material and the companies weren't happy about that. YouTube had to prepare for potential lawsuits and funding a large team of lawyers and legal advisors was extremely costly.

YouTube was spiraling out of control and it was all due to rapid success. The growing traffic was countered by growing costs that were too difficult to manage in such a short period of time. As a result, the founders started looking to sell.

Google Steps In

Despite the resounding success YouTube enjoyed, the costs of maintaining a continually growing infrastructure and copyright infringement lawsuits were too much for a company that lacked income. Bankruptcy was on the horizon, but the platform's quick rise to fame had attracted Google's attention.

In 2005-2006 Google was a major player, dominating the Internet. The search engine company attempted to create its own video sharing platform called "Google Video", but it failed to gain any serious traction and it was discontinued. So when YouTube began looking for a buyer, Google rushed with an offer of $1,65 billion. This acquisition marked another major milestone in the history of the Internet, YouTube, and Google.

Once YouTube went under Google's control, the search engine giant continued investing and developing the platform instead of absorbing it. In retrospect, this was a great strategy as YouTube is now generating roughly 10% of Google's revenue. Google had the financial power to minimize the risk of lawsuits by negotiating with the entertainment industry to allow YouTube to host certain copyrighted material. Users could not use various songs and footage to create their videos without the risk of having their content removed. However, this came with the condition of Google removing thousands of copyrighted videos that didn't fall under the fair use agreement that was negotiated.

As Google continued their efforts in taking YouTube to the next level, the focus went on expansion. The year of 2007 represented a new beginning. YouTube was launched in nine other countries together and a mobile version of the site was created as well. Google introduced in-video ads, significantly increasing the income generated by the platform and they created a partner program to stimulate content creators.

Note: Did you know that the first Rickroll happened in 2007? And did you know that the Queen of England launched her own YouTube channel that same year? It was a crazy year!

YouTube was expanding faster than ever. In 2008 and 2009, a series of improvements were made to the platform. The analytics tool was launched, captions and annotations became available, and by December 2008 720p HD was enabled. As the quality of videos increased, and more quality of life features were introduced, YouTube began attracting the attention of entertainment giants like MGM, CBS, and Disney, as well as governments and state-run institutions.

Google signed deals with MGM and CBS to bring their full-length programming to YouTube. The US Congress and the Vatican were among the first governmental powers to launch their own channels. YouTube was becoming a true social media force. By the end of 2009, YouTube announced that the platform reached one billion views per day. This impressive rate would double by May 2010 as the video quality was raised further to 1080p and a new Individual Video Partnership was launched.

Redesign and Growth

The year of 2010 marked the beginning of a new age, as Chad Hurley, one of the original founders, decided to step down as YouTube's CEO and function only in an advisory capacity. Salar Kamangar became the new chief executive of the company in October.

But major changes were already happening in March 2010, as YouTube was relaunched with a new, simpler design. The goal was to improve user experience to increase the time spent on the platform by simplifying the interface and making it more user-friendly. The result was a 1 billion views per day increase every year. In

2010 YouTube recorded two billion daily views and that rate doubled by 2012. YouTube was the dominant video-sharing platform in the US.

In 2011, more design changes occurred and the logo was modified for the first time. However, it was 2012 that proved to be a big year. That's when the Gangnam Style music video broke the Internet by quickly gathering over a billion views. The view count was unprecedented on YouTube and it is partially responsible for the future change in how the view count algorithm works. Since then, Youtube started ranking videos based on how much time viewers spent watching them, instead of just counting views.

Until 2013, YouTube continued on its path to attract more users through its simplicity and by integrating itself with other social media platforms. Google's own Google+ social networking platform was a prime example of this trend. At the time, YouTube could be accessed from the Google+ interface that was also integrated into the Chrome browser.

With the upgraded interface and the changes made to the ranking algorithm, new types of videos started emerging around 2012-2014. Longer videos usually translated to better ranking because viewers spent significantly more time on them. This led to the rise of "top 10" video compilations and "let's play" videos. PewDiePie (Felix Kjellberg) started out in 2010 with horror games gameplay videos and by 2012 he gathered a following of one million subscribers. By 2013, his channel had the highest number of subscribers on YouTube.

In 2014, the feature expansion project continued with the launch of 60 frames per second videos. In addition, YouTube started taking a new turn by seeking new methods of monetization. As a result, YouTube RED was introduced, nowadays known as YouTube Premium, which was/is a paid version of the platform, but without any ads and the ability to access videos offline.

YouTube maintained this path until 2021 without making any more drastic changes. Nonetheless, the video-sharing platform is barely recognizable when comparing it to itself back in 2005. A great deal of today's traffic data is eaten up by YouTube and the millions of people who watch and upload videos. In 2020, due to the coronavirus pandemic, YouTube's traffic increased so much that the European Union had to ask the platform to cut back on its bandwidth to leave more room for medical services.

Changing Your Perspective of YouTube

YouTube is no longer just a video-sharing website. It is a social media platform and a search engine at the same time. Video content is one of the best methods of sending a message to your audience. Whether it's for entertainment purposes, company branding, advertising, or teaching, YouTube is a powerful way of delivering information.

The video format is increasingly more popular and it's becoming a favorite for Google's search engine algorithms. Because of how frequently quality video content is shared via social media, Google is taking notice of it. If one of your goals is to grow your presence on the Internet, you can use YouTube videos to improve your brand's search engine optimization (SEO). In other words, provided you create a video and share it through YouTube by using great titles, accurate descriptions, and appropriate tags, Google will boost your ranking. Therefore, setting up a YouTube channel isn't just for gamers and vloggers anymore. If you want to run a successful business in any field, you can show off your brand, services, or products by making and sharing YouTube videos.

In addition to marketing yourself or your business directly, YouTube is probably the best platform you can use to teach others how to solve a problem. By demonstrating certain concepts related to your business via YouTube videos, you can establish yourself as an authority on the subject. This might not boost your business from the start, but over time it will show potential customers that you know what you're talking about and you have a lot of value to offer. Some of that value is present in your free YouTube videos, which leads to branding.

Videos transmit a lot of information quickly. A few seconds of video content are often more valuable than a page of text. The same thing goes for branding. People like visuals. It's as simple as that. It's much harder to grab someone's attention or convey a specific emotion or mood through text. Whatever you're promoting, video is the right way to do it and with YouTube's smooth integration into other social media platforms it's easier than ever to build your brand. Once you create a video, you can spread it easily. It's not locked away on YouTube. You can add to your Facebook timeline, share it on Twitter, and even email it.

All of this is possible on a small budget. The main purpose of YouTube was always to allow users share their videos. It wasn't intended for professional actors and movie producers. You can create good-quality videos that offer a lot of value to the viewer with a minimal investment in some basic video equipment and editing software.

The Inner Workings of YouTube

YouTube's growth and popularity boils down to a user-friendly interface and powerful backend engineering. The platform accepts a variety of different video formats such as MP4, AVI, MOV, and WMV, making it easy for anyone to upload their content no matter what capturing and editing software they use. This advantage extends to the ability to embed the video content on your own website.

As mentioned earlier, YouTube is an excellent marketing and branding tool, but it doesn't have to be the only tool you use. You can spread your content throughout social media, but YouTube also allows you to easily embed and play it to your audience from the comfort of your website. By using some basic HTML code (that you can find and copy-paste), you can embed the video you uploaded to YouTube to your own website. This implies installing a YouTube player on your website, which is a process that doesn't take more than a couple of minutes. But why bother when you can simply host your own video? Hosting a video requires bandwidth and if you have more than a few videos, you're going to end up spending a lot of money, especially if you want to offer your audience full HD quality. By using this method, YouTube will handle the hard part of the job for you. All you need to do is link your website to the platform.

While embedding videos is a great way to spread your wings over the Internet, most people will come across your content by searching for it. Since YouTube is also a search engine like Google, it works in similar ways to connect the user to specific content. YouTube's search algorithms are certainly complex but know enough to make them work in our favor. Whenever you're searching for video content, the algorithms use a number of variables to decide what results to display for you. Those results are ranked based on those variables. It's impossible to manipulate all of them, but the most important ones are the title of the video, its description, tags, and thumbnail. Keep that in mind when you upload a video. Decide the title and the rest of the metadata based on the kind of content you're sharing. Make it as easy as possible for people to find your content by focusing on specific keywords they might use.

YouTube used to base its ranking system on the number of views a video had. However, that was changed due to a number of vulnerabilities. Nowadays, the quality of the content is determined based on how much time people spend watching the video. Therefore, if the majority of viewers stop watching a thirty-minute video after just one minute, the algorithm starts thinking that there's something wrong with the content. That simple metric suggests that the uploader titled the video inaccurately, failed to provide an adequate description, or that the content doesn't offer anything of value to most users. On the other hand, if the majority of viewers watch the video close to the end, it means the metadata is accurate and the content offers value. As a result, the video receives a high ranking. That being said, we assume there are other ranking factors at play, but the algorithm is complex, in constant change, and YouTube doesn't want to reveal its secrets.

Where does it all go? Is my content safe? These are some of the most common questions about all the data that goes to YouTube. Data security is a valid concern, but rest assured, all the videos you upload to YouTube are stored and protected for you. In essence, it's impossible to lose anything. Google is in charge of safely storing everything that's on YouTube by using their massive data centers. These data centers, which are spread around the world, house thousands of servers that store your content and manage everything that goes on on the search engine. A typical data center is strictly controlled to ensure optimal computer operating temperatures. The servers themselves are regularly maintained, and multiple ones are used to backing up your data. Even if something goes wrong with a server, your content won't be lost. Furthermore, data centers are connected to each other and they communicate with each other. Once you upload your video, it's actually sent to the closest data center. When someone clicks on it to watch it, the video is sent from that data center to the one that's closest to the user. This ensures rapid access to the content, but it also means your data is kept safe. If something goes wrong with the data center itself, like a fire breaking out, all of the data stored there is sent to other data centers.

That being said, YouTube takes care of your content, makes it easily accessible if you satisfy the search engine's requirements, and whatever you upload is protected.

More Than Leisure

While YouTube started out as a website where you could share videos with your friends, it evolved into so much more. For many, YouTube remains an entertainment platform that hosts funny cat videos, ridiculous car crashes, conspiracy theories, and music. However, the platform must not be underestimated for its educational potential.

YouTube has a lot of value to offer in education. You can find anything from instructional videos on how to fix a leaky pipe to university-level machine learning lectures. Out of the hundreds of hours of video content that is being uploaded every day, we can find educational content on any topic we can think of. The thirst for easily accessible knowledge has also pushed a number of NGOs to offer entire collections of lessons and lectors for free.

Many programmers, artists, and writers start out by learning from those video tutorials and lessons on YouTube. As a result, schools are starting to integrate the video platform and specifically a number of educational YouTube channels into their own curriculum. Many professors started recording their own lectures so that they can share them for free with anyone who's curious and willing to learn but maybe lack the funds to get a formal degree.

YouTube is flexible enough to allow anyone with knowledge and skill on a certain topic to teach others. Content developers, teachers, tradesmen, and hobbyists alike post videos on a regular basis on every topic you can think of. Whether it's leatherworking, fitness, or astrophysics, the entire world has something to learn thanks to YouTube. This very same flexibility brought TED (technology education and design) conferences on the mainstream stage. With over 2,000 free lectures presented by leaders from every field, viewers can learn from the comfort of their own homes without spending a cent.

YouTube is leading the charge, changing the education system from a strict, rigid format, to an open easy-to-access model that works for everyone. As life starts getting in the way of many, it's of utmost importance to still have access to education. YouTube offers this access allowing even those with limited budgets or full-time jobs to learn a new skill through bite-sized video content instead of hours after hours of traditional schooling. Knowledge has never been easier to attain than it is now. All it takes is a bit of motivation and minimal digital know-how to access the right educational content.

Chapter 2 - What Makes YouTube Unique?

Social media is everywhere and it is true when they say that if you don't have social media, it is as if you don't exist. It's not just about people using it to communicate with each other, to make friends, and make themselves seen. Companies use social media to advertise themselves, to find new employees, to establish their audience, and to grow their business. Politicians use social media to easily give the people access to their agendas, but also to launch their election campaigns. Musicians, photographers, various crafters, game developers, and others use social media to establish their presence and to reach out to their audience. But social media is ever-changing, and no matter what your business is, you should make a call and decide which type of social media is right for your business, and which platform can meet all your expectations.

There is no type of social media yet that can beat direct communication, but some of them can make your business sound and appear more personal. Through various platforms, you can advertise yourself and also reach out to your audience on a more personal level. This interaction between you as a creative drive behind your product (be it video, music, or simply a commercial for a product) and your audience is important and should be maintained. All social media will allow you to do this, but it is up to you to decide which of the platforms will balance out your online presence the best. In the end, you cannot focus only on the audience, you also have to think about the quality of your material, the design of your brand, the monetization options, and what you have to offer.

This chapter will show you the differences between various social networks and how they compare with YouTube. You will also learn why you should choose YouTube and how to grow your business through it. But in the end, don't forget to have fun. Whether you strive to become a YouTube star, or if you just look to expand your business, using YouTube shouldn't feel like doing chores.

YouTube vs. Other Social Media Platforms

Before you can choose the social media platform that suits your needs the best, let's see what is out there, what choices you have, what can each of them offer, and why you should choose YouTube! Many people are surprised to learn that YouTube is considered a social network, but the truth is, it has all the elements of one. However, YouTube is a unique social network and a perfect choice for everyone who is trying to communicate their message through video. But let's not get ahead of ourselves, and let's see what other platforms have to offer, their pros and cons, and how they perform in comparison to YouTube. This way we will answer the question of why YouTube is such a unique place on the World Wide Web.

Facebook

Probably the best-known social network out there is Facebook. And it is a great platform because it offers so much to individuals as well as businesses. It incorporates almost all media formats, such as text, audio, and video. Facebook is used by a large segment of the global population, and such a big audience attracts many businesses to the platform. However, despite Facebook offering special sales and marketing tools to business owners, it is almost never the first choice for business owners. This is due to it not being the best option for the development of a brand. Businesses should always establish their brand, grow it, and use Facebook only to increase their reach. Facebook is a platform that can bring the awareness of your business to the next level because it allows you to be seen and for your content to be shared among millions of its users.

For videographers, Facebook is probably an ideal second choice. Just as any other platform, it will allow you access to a wide audience, but when it actually comes to videos themselves, Facebook often falls short. This is precisely because this platform tries to incorporate so many media in itself. Just like a Jack of all trades, Facebook is a master of none. It cannot offer high-quality service to videographers. Facebook's many users like the simplicity of having it all in one place, and for their needs, Facebook came up with "Facebook Watch", a separate tab within the App, or website, for all the video content lovers out there.

Facebook Watch offers easy access to videos that were published on Facebook, however, there is a trick to it. A video needs to come from a very reputable page, such as the ones with more than 5,000 followers. If you are new to making videos and you are just beginning to spread your influence, you would have to dedicate a lot of time and money to become one of the reputable pages in order for your videos to be seen. This is something that is limiting you as a creator. Ask yourself if you even have enough time to dedicate to both creating quality content for your video and managing your social presence, all for only one platform?

Facebook Watch was created in 2017, with the intention to offer the viewers only the videos which were commissioned by Facebook. That means that in its early stages, the users of these platforms were not able to share their videos. The very next year Facebook Watch opened up to all of its users. But it was always intended to be a limited platform with a limited offer. Because of this, once everyone was able to upload their videos the platform itself had to change. The problem is, that Facebook Watch is still changing, and very often too. Constant updates and tweaks to the algorithm are what a creator has to deal with if he chooses to use Facebook Watch. This unpredictability of the platform is off-putting for many of its users.

In 2019, Facebook started offering its users a percentage of the money made from the ads that are played during their videos. This was a great change, however, the unpredictability of Facebook's algorithm makes it a very unreliable option for anyone who wants to earn money from videos. Some users have been complaining that one month they would earn a decent amount of money, but the next month they wouldn't see any revenues at all. And all of this just because Facebook suddenly decided to make some changes to how their algorithm works. These updates forced content developers to adapt continuously. While earning money using this platform is possible, it demands you to constantly keep track and update your marketing tactics to be able to keep up with Facebook. This means you would waste your time on managing your page more than creating quality video content for your audience.

Many people ask why not combine Facebook and YouTube, why not cross-post? This is always an option and something you should definitely consider doing. But even if you opt for cross-posting you would have to decide which social media would be your main video sharing platform. Facebook works completely differently than YouTube. Most of the time people don't search for videos intentionally when browsing Facebook. It comes as recommended on their newsfeed, and Facebook utilizes silent autoplay. This means that your video would have to be designed specifically to catch the attention of a person scrolling down his news-feed. A person is less likely to click on a video on Facebook if it doesn't have a flashy or colorful thumbnail or autoplay which would attract the eye quickly. Facebook users tend to prefer visual stimulation to auditory, and they tend to keep the sound off while watching a video. If you want to create videos that rely on sound, maybe you should consider Facebook as your secondary option. Creating video content that caters to both Facebook and YouTube at the same time is nearly impossible.

Unlike Facebook Watch, YouTube is considered a consistent platform. That doesn't mean YouTube's algorithms never change, but some parts of it became codified. This means that YouTube is generally a more stable option that will strive to bring you equal revenues even if there are some changes implemented. YouTube is reliable when compared to Facebook Watch, but it does attract a different kind of audience. Its search engine is so advanced that newer generations are starting to use it as an alternative to Google.

YouTube is meant to be used as a separate app or website. As such, the platform is completely dedicated to videos, which means it will guarantee quality delivery to your audience. YouTube users are many and even though its algorithm is capable of suggesting videos based on the users' viewing history, it is mostly designed for a direct search. But this is not limiting at all. This means your videos will reach the audience that is interested in the type of videos you are making, and not just anyone. While it is true it's harder to reach new viewers, it does spare you from negative comments and ratings coming from people who were not interested in seeing your video in the first place. This is something that Facebook doesn't offer you. Another great aspect of YouTube, in comparison to Facebook, is that you can make the content as flashy as you want, or you could make it purely an auditory experience, it doesn't matter. In the end, it will always reach the right audience for you.

The major advantage of YouTube is that it can be shared on all other websites. It can be embedded in blog posts, news articles, newsletters, or it can be shared on other social media platforms, even on Facebook. The success of a video posted on Facebook purely depends on its news feed algorithm. But when it comes to YouTube, the content creator has full control of its success through SEO. This is because Google indexes YouTube videos. In other words, your video will pop-up as a Google search result, while a video posted on Facebook won't. That means that millions of people who use Google every day can become your potential viewers. YouTube is not as limiting as Facebook and ultimately it is a better choice. Your videos can be shared, can reach millions and millions of users, can bring you a stable income and you can fully control the quality of their display as well as their success.

Twitter

Twitter is a social network used for what is known as "Microblogging". It allows its user to post only up to 280 characters, but this number is occasionally increasing (it started from 140 characters). It is an easy-to-use platform with a newsfeed that will show you "tweets", or posts, from the people you follow. You can reply to their tweets, you can post your own, or you can re-tweet or share other people's tweets. Twitter is a great way to communicate your thoughts and messages in a very direct manner. It is used by various types of people from politicians, scientists, influencers, institutions, and businesses. It is a great way to reach your audience and express yourself. But if you are a video content creator, you may find Twitter extremely limiting. While it does allow linking your videos from other platforms, Twitter itself is not a good choice as the main platform from which to share your videos. This is because the platform allows very short formats, and the maximum length of a video is 10 minutes. However, this is available only to companies that want to share their video ads. Tweets in the form of a video are even shorter, as the maximal length is 2 minutes and 20 seconds.

That being said, Twitter is constantly evolving and changing its rules, and with the further development of technology, this platform pushes its limits. Video length might be increased in the future. Twitter is, primarily, designed for very short and direct content. This shouldn't discourage you from using Twitter at all. It is still a great place to share links to your YouTube videos, to spread your brand's presence, and attract an audience. Because of Twitter's time limits, videos designed for this platform are easy and quick to make. For example, you can create a preview of your main YouTube video and tweet it as a commercial. Twitter is perfect for commercializing your YouTube videos because the links can be embedded within a tweet and look as if it's part of it. Aesthetically pleasing and easily accessible links are a major plus!

TikTok

Similar to Twitter's microblogging narrative, TikTok is a micro-vlogging platform. It is a social network, completely dedicated to short videos with a maximum length of up to three minutes. TikTok is also available only to smartphone users as it is basically a smartphone app developed for IOS and Android operating systems. Nevertheless, the content shared on this platform reaches over 2 billion users worldwide. It is a powerful app and its popularity is skyrocketing. More and more companies, as well as small business owners, are using TikTok to promote their products and businesses in a creative way.

For a full-time video content developer, TikTok is a very limiting platform. The fact that it works only on IOS and Android smartphones will influence your ability to reach certain audiences. Furthermore, TikTok users form an unreliable audience as they are usually in the search of and quick entertainment. In addition, TikTok doesn't offer a share of the revenues to content creators and people who earn money through this social network do it mostly by advertising products and directing the traffic to online stores. However, this is a tactic a

YouTuber could also use. Just like with Twitter you can create short and catchy commercials for your main YouTube channel, and use TikTok to direct the audience to it.

Instagram

Instagram is home to many businesses, influencers, bloggers, and vloggers because it uses stunning and expressive visuals to attract the audience in order to promote products or content. This is why Instagram should be very carefully considered by video makers. Like Twitter and TikTok, Instagram is best suited for short and quick content that catches the eye of the audience. But the advantage of Instagram is that if your audience is younger than 40, they are most likely using this app.

Originally, the app was created for smartphones to share pictures, but nowadays Instagram strives to cater to everyone and the possibility of creating, uploading, and viewing videos was introduced too. These are usually selfie-style videos, perfect for vloggers and influencers who want to make a quick promotional material and direct the audience to their main platform.

That being said, Instagram should never be used purely for vlogging. As the networks described above, it is a limiting platform that allows short videos and limited content. If you are using it, remember that visual stimulation is the most important part of Instagram and you should focus your effort on making separate short videos only for Instagram. This app is to be used only for cross-posting and marketing. So why should you opt for Instagram above all others? Because of the size of the audience. If you have doubts about whether to use Instagram, Facebook, TikTok, or Twitter, simply go with Instagram because it's rarely a mistake. But remember, this app is not an alternative to YouTube, but only an additional marketing and outreach platform.

The Verdict

As you can see, there is no real alternative to YouTube. Facebook Watch came close to making a worthy competitor, but ultimately it failed because it was trying to cater to the demands of its whole user base. YouTube remains the only social media platform that is optimal for video content. Whether you want to be a vlogger, influencer, create intriguing gaming or science-related content, or if you want to talk about books, perform interviews, or promote your music, YouTube is the perfect place. It even offers you various ways to communicate with your audience. But just like any social network out there, YouTube is evolving and constantly changing. It follows the latest trends and who knows what the future will bring. Remember that YouTube is the second most used search engine out there after Google and many people use it on a regular basis for entertainment or to learn something new. The average time spent on YouTube is constantly increasing. This gives you, a video content creator, the freedom to choose the length of your videos, their content, and their visual and auditory appeal. This is why YouTube is so unique.

Why is YouTube the Best Choice for You Right Now?

YouTube is probably one of the most successful social media platforms out there because it benefits not only its developers but also its users. Whether you're a simple user or a content creator, or even a brand or a company, YouTube has something to offer you.

As a content creator, YouTube will reward you no matter if your channel is successful or if it fails. Instagram and Facebook, for example, do not have the option of direct payment to the content creator. However, YouTube does. To some degree, the platform offers you protection. But the compensation you might get from YouTube is not always money. Sometimes it comes in the form of networking. YouTube is famous for connecting you with professionals in the industry because YouTube strives to reward quality videos. Otherwise, everyone would make low-quality content just so they could make money from views. If the content is low quality, the users will leave, and so would the companies that pay for commercials, and the platform would fail. The better the quality of your content, the more compensation you would get.

Another reason why YouTube is the best choice for content creators is that it is the only social media platform that rewards creativity, but it is also completely driven by creativity. Just as Instagram is a home for photographers who try to put themselves on the scene, YouTube is a platform for video and audio content creators. This means that if you're a filmmaker, but you don't have the access to the big industry yet, YouTube is the perfect place where you could start. It will not only allow you to store your videos so you could show them off, but it would also compensate you for the hard work you put into making those videos. YouTube is doing this so it could mobilize talent that is usually underrepresented. It is your talent that attracts the users to the platform, and YouTube recognizes it.

Everyone on YouTube gets the same opportunity to present himself, and succeed. YouTube doesn't discriminate, and the platform allows a healthy amount of competition. The platform itself will not close itself to musicians because there are too many music creators out there. It is up to you, the content creator, to make your videos shine and attract the audience.

That being said, the most important reason why YouTube is the best social media platform for you is that it allows you to nurture your passion, to learn, grow, change, shape yourself and while doing this you can even start earning. You can either use YouTube as a side business, which will give you that extra income you could use. Or you can make YouTube your platform of choice on which you would launch your career. This is why a "YouTuber" became a profession, and you can even pay your taxes by signing yourself as a YouTuber. There are many stories out there of people who quit their 9 to 5 office jobs just so they could pursue their passions and become

YouTubers. There is truth to that saying " if you do what you love, you won't work a single day". And many would say that YouTube is oversaturated, that everyone is becoming a YouTuber or an influencer. Some even doubt you could earn money by doing what everyone else is doing. But this is simply not true. You can still succeed on YouTube, even if your passion is largely represented already. You just need to find your own voice, do it in your own unique way and people will want to watch your videos.

To the young generations, YouTube stars are as famous as any rock star out there. They gather their fans into tight-knit communities and these fans are their primary audience. You don't even need to have millions of subscribers to experience this phenomenon. But remember that YouTube is about healthy competition, and anyone can become successful if they have something of value to offer. It's easy to say "be unique", or "just keep pursuing your passion and you will make it". However, YouTube reached a certain point of maturity, technologically and content-wise. It is not easy to become a hit overnight, but it's not quite impossible either. There are many ways to make yourself noticed. From offering high-quality content, which is probably the most important aspect of a YouTube channel, to creating collaborations with other YouTubers who could attract new audiences to your channel. In order to succeed on YouTube, you should develop a proper marketing strategy, or maybe even think about hiring a specialist who could help you push yourself out there. Having a plan and following it will eventually yield good results.

Using YouTube to Grow Business

You don't have to be a YouTuber to use this platform for your business purposes. Like any other social platform, YouTube is an excellent way to grow and expand your business. It will allow you to reach not only new customers but also the people with who you can work and collaborate. In other words, YouTube is an excellent networking platform for any kind of business out there. This is simply because, in the 21st century, social media marketing is the most important form of marketing we have. It completely replaces the traditional methods of advertising, and every business needs an online presence. We already discussed how YouTube, besides being a social media, is also the second most used search engine. Google is also indexing YouTube videos, and if done properly, your video ad can be among the first results Google displays.

Here are a few benefits of using YouTube to grow your business:

1. **Reach a bigger audience!** YouTube has billions of users and hundreds of hours of videos uploaded daily. This means that this platform puts at your disposal a huge audience that can potentially become your customers or fans. Of course, YouTube won't do the marketing for you, and you still have to think about how to drive that audience to come to visit your channel. There are many ways to attract people, but keep in mind that everyone wants to see quality videos. Once you focus on that, you can start generating a high number of views as videos with high numbers attract even more people and potential customers. The best way to do this is to share your YouTube videos through other social network platforms such as Facebook or Twitter.

2. **Generate Traffic!** Yes, you can use YouTube to generate traffic to your

website. Simply place the link to your website in the description of your video ad and you will gain clicks. People are curious, and if your video attracts their attention, they'll want to find out more directly from your website. Another way to generate traffic through YouTube is to collaborate with vloggers and influencers. Find a suitable YouTuber who you think would present your product or your service the best. They will work hard to spark the interest in their own audience for your product, and that audience would happily click on the link which would lead them to your website.

3. **Increase your Google presence!** YouTube is part of Google. Google's search engine algorithm started considering videos a valuable and trustworthy source of information, and YouTube videos are highly ranked. But in order to make this feature work for you, you will have to follow a few rules. You will need to mind the use of keywords and create your titles, hashtags, and video descriptions accordingly. You need to organize and categorize your content properly, and if you have a blog on your

website, make the videos a part of them. If your video content complements the text, Google would rank it even higher.

4. **The economic value of YouTube is unmatched!** Not only is creating a YouTube ad cheaper, but it is also much faster in generating traffic. The traditional marketing methods take time. They need to reach a wide audience but they are limited as they are not available to a large enough audience. YouTube will reach the targeted audience immediately and you will see the first results in no time. Time is money, and the faster you reach your audience, the faster you will start developing your business.

5. **Stay in touch with your audience!** YouTube, just as any other social network platform, will allow you to communicate with your audience through comments. But it will offer you even more than that. You can ask your viewers to be a part of your campaign by recording their reviews of your products and services. Make them feel that there is a human behind the videos and make them a part of what you are doing.

6. **Build brand awareness!** Through contact with your audience, you can raise brand awareness and loyalty. But for this, you would need to create a special connection with your viewers. You can do this easily through a series of initiatives you can start on YouTube. People love social initiatives and they will want to know your company's stance on many of the modern social issues. Research the modern trends and share your views on them. It can be about climate change, Pride month, animal welfare, and any other pressing matters. Organize charities, lotteries, and give away prizes related to your business. You can even opt to give special discounts to your YouTube followers.

Developing and expanding your business through social media is a fun task, and doing it through YouTube makes it engaging, interesting, modern, and very economic. Remember that YouTube is not only a place where you will display your ads. It is a fun, ever-growing community that appreciates communication between professionals and users. YouTube is an awesome place through which you can show the human side of your business. Show the face that stands behind the brand, act natural, joyful and share your happiness and emotions with your audience. This will increase their loyalty and YouTube will improve your ranking.

Using YouTube for Fun

YouTube is popular because once you create your account and your YouTube channel, you will have total freedom to decide what to do with it and how to promote it if you choose to do so. Some people want to become internet famous, but others want to keep their videos private, and maybe share them with certain friends and family members.

There is no right or wrong way of using YouTube. In the end, it all comes down to personal preferences. Some people will never make their own channel and won't post their videos. They use YouTube to enjoy the content other people have to offer. These people are called viewers and they are attracted to YouTube for various reasons. The platform offers them quality content for free, and easy access to their favorite videos. They can keep track of their favorite content creators, follow them and enjoy their new videos as soon as they're posted. There are even options that will enable you to receive a special notification whenever your favorite YouTuber uploads a new video. YouTube users are also given access to new music videos, movie trailers, and popular brand reviews. Although YouTube strives to cultivate the unrepresented talent, most of the famous names out there keep their presence on YouTube too. This is because they recognize the advantages of this social network and use it to promote themselves and their work. But most of all, the viewers love YouTube because of its various possibilities. Through the video content, they can have fun, amuse themselves by watching various gameplays, cartoons, or any content design to make them laugh. But they can also watch documentaries, interviews with famous people, and learn about the science or social problems of our world. There is everything for every person's taste on YouTube, and it's so easy to access its content.

That being said, YouTube is also fun for creative people who want to make their presence known - the YouTubers! Being a YouTuber and sharing your videos is a fun experience. It gives you the feeling that your opinions matter, that your talent is finally being seen and that your products are reaching their targeted audience. It is a satisfying feeling to know you are out there, and people appreciate what you are doing. To creators, YouTube gives freedom to express themselves and put themselves out there. But it also gives them the opportunity to earn money, to be discovered, to find business partners or potential new employees. The possibilities are endless and this is why the platform is popular and growing exponentially.

Section 2:
Starting Your Channel

Chapter 3 -
Choosing a Niche

Being a YouTuber means creating satisfying content for your audience. However, "audience" is a very vast term and you can have as much of it as there are users on YouTube. It is impossible to keep them all satisfied and you should never strive to do so. Instead, you should find a niche for your YouTube channel. All businesses work using this model. They find a niche market and they establish themselves as the dominant power within that selected niche. Although there are some success stories about people who managed to create the audience for their niche. This is very unlikely and you should not risk it. Instead, you should always strive to work within a niche that already has its own audience. In this chapter, you will learn how to pick a niche filled with potential and how to develop a successful YouTube channel around it.

Identifying Your Goals

Choosing a niche is no easy task. There are so many options out there. Some of them may be your passion and you might already have a vague idea of how you would develop your business from it. However, YouTube is a very unique social network and you will first have to ask yourself what it is that you want to achieve with your own channel. Setting goals for your YouTube channel is an extremely important part of planning your future business. With a clear vision of what you want to achieve, it will be easier to decide further steps you need to take in order to succeed. While some people have a vision and know exactly what their goals are, it might help them to re-evaluate their decisions and see if those goals are achievable in the first place. Other people don't really have a clear vision and they are going to need some brainstorming sessions in order to put it on paper.

To succeed you need to understand that your YouTube channel needs to offer value to others. Although it might be about you, or something that you do, all of your videos will be made for your audience. You need to ask yourself who do you want to help or entertain, who is your target audience? This question is probably the most important one you should ask yourself before choosing your niche. Your audience is what makes your presence on YouTube a success or a failure. After all, they are your subscribers, and the more of them you have, the more likely you would be to succeed. Determine not only the interests of your audience but also the whole demographics. This will later help you shape your videos into a narrative suitable for the type of people you want to cater to. Decide the age, sex, and even the location of the people you want to reach out to.

Now is the time to decide if you want to make your subscribers laugh, think, or learn a new skill. This will help you further determine the tone of your videos as well as their topics. Every video will make its viewers feel something, and you are in full control to decide what that feeling will be. Do you want to do comedy videos or general entertainment, or maybe you want to discuss burning social questions, educate your viewers on technical topics, or maybe show them your unique talents.

The next step is to determine the skills that you need to make your videos likable. Ask yourself what is it in you that you have to offer to the world? Do you like to talk and know how to keep an interesting conversation about various topics? Do you sing, dance, or play an instrument? Or maybe you are a gamer or a painter. Once you determine the special skill that will set you apart, it will be much easier to determine your niche. Remember that even if you have just one skill, let's say you play an instrument, you don't have to create a channel where you will simply show off that skill. You could also strive to give YouTube lessons to beginners, or teach them the history of your favorite instrument, talk about the theory behind music, and react to other YouTube videos of people who play your chosen instrument. The options are endless and you don't have to limit yourself. Combining different types of videos, but keeping them in the same niche will yield the best results.

If you set the goals for your YouTube channel from the start you will have a clearer image of what your niche should be. Even if you already know the niche in which you will work, it is always useful to have the goals in front of you as they will help you develop your channel properly. You will have a clear vision of what skills you have to offer, and what skills you need to improve to better yourself and your channel. Having a successful YouTube channel is all about keeping up with the trends, developing yourself, and constantly learning about new methods you could implement to start a successful YouTube channel. However, that doesn't mean the first goals you set have to be set in stone. You can change your goals as time passes and set new ones. Keep it as an interesting game and regard your goals as achievements. Once you achieve your first 1,000 subscribers set a new goal to reach 10,000. Set goals about the context of your video, your marketing approach, or even about attracting sponsors to your channel. Make a collaboration video your next goal. Keeping the goals alive will make maintaining a successful YouTube channel fun, challenging, and most importantly rewarding.

Why Choose a Niche?

Chances are you have many skills and have a lot to say to your audience. You might ask yourself why you need to limit yourself within the confines of a niche, and why is it important to choose just one among so many things you are good at? While there is no rule that would forbid you from making content on various topics, or about showing off your different skills, there are some setbacks to it. The main one would be your audience. You want to create a base of followers, your loyal viewers, who would come back to your channel because they know what content to expect. But not everyone will like everything that you do, and keeping them all happy is impossible. Therefore, sticking to one niche will make it much easier for you to please your subscribers. Remember that you can always have multiple channels and create content for different niches. But you would have to work twice as hard to maintain multiple channels and create quality content that would engage your audience and keep them happy. Having multiple niches spread across different channels may wear you out quickly and soon you will find out you don't have enough energy.

The unwritten rule of making a successful YouTube channel is posting at least one video per week. If you have, lets say, three different channels, you would need to create three videos per week. Do you think you can make three high quality content videos in one week? While this is quite possible, if you are just starting your own channel, you need to collect some experience first. It is better to keep yourself focused on only one channel and on one niche, at least in the beginning. Later you might develop more channels, or implement other niches into your existing one. However, even then you would have to be careful not to put off your existing audience and lose subscribers. Research niches that work together the best and evaluate how your subscribers react to them. Research will give you a general idea about what audiences are looking for.

Introducing the Various Worlds in YouTube

There are many factors that determine the popularity of various YouTube niches and categories. One of them is geography - the location of your channel, as well as the geographic location of your subscribers. For example, one of the most popular YouTubers out there is PewDiePie. He is originally from Sweden but he is based in England. However, his YouTube channel is registered in the U.S. This is what allowed him to gain millions of subscribers and reach the top.

An audience's interests depend on their country. Some are more interested in channels which deliver their content in their native language, while others are open to international channels. The U.S. is by far the largest YouTube audience, and in general, English speaking YouTubers have higher chances of succeeding.

Aside from geography, the category you choose will play an enormous influence on your success. The type of content you create will determine how many possible subscribers you can have. Entertainment is by far the most successful category. It is followed by gaming, which we can say belongs in the same entertainment category. Next up is the "how to" category with various do it yourself and life hacks channels that regularly create quality content. These three categories alone are consumed by the vast majority of viewers.

You should keep this information in mind when trying to decide which niche to focus on in your own YouTube channel. But these categories are very general and broad. It doesn't help much to narrow down your ideal niche. So, if you still have trouble deciding on what to focus, here is a list of the most popular and highest earning niches you could consider:

1. **Vlogging**: A vlog refers to a video blog or video log. When a regular person picks up a camera and records the events of his every-day life, he is creating a vlog. Vlogging became popular because it caters to the social animal that dwells in all of us. Getting to know other people by observing their lives gives us satisfaction and the inspiration we need to better ourselves. But it could also simply entertain us by indulging our voyeuristic needs. Vloggers are many and in order to be successful in this niche, you could narrow it down to what makes you a

unique individual. There are family vloggers, travel vloggers, musician vloggers, and so on.

2. **Tech**: Tech is something that is continuously developing and new products are launched every day. This means you have an opportunity to pick a niche that will never dry out. However, tech is also a very saturated niche and it is best to focus your efforts on a certain type of tech. You can choose anything between computer processors, cameras, smartphones, house appliances, TVs, drones, cloud services, and anything else that has some connection to technology. You can do product reviews, talk about their development, or make videos that will teach other people how to properly use a certain product. Tech is a general niche that can be broken down into hundreds of sub-niches. This is a good thing because you have the opportunity to start talking about something new that nobody else had covered before.

3. **Tutorials**: Are you a make-up specialist? Or maybe an excellent cook? Perhaps you're a skilled plumber or you're excellent with cars. Teach people

how to unclog a pipe, change their oil, or replace a tire. YouTube is frequently used for educational purposes, so start teaching your audience how to do something you're good at. Tutorials are especially popular among the younger generation that is just getting their independence. Be that reliable guy or girl on the internet on which they can rely. That being said, you should focus on a specific skill. Talking about beauty and car engines on the same channel will quickly alienate parts of your audience.

4. **Healthy lifestyle**: You may be proud of how you turned around your life and transformed yourself from a couch potato to a healthy guru. Help other people lose weight and inspire them with your own transformation story. Show off your diet, teach your audience how to prepare a healthy meal. Set an example for others by showing them your workout routine. Health is another broad niche, but it is one of the most popular ones and it has a lot to offer. All you need to do is find something that hasn't been done to death or present your content in a unique, creative way.

5. **Storytelling videos**: If you have the amazing ability to tell stories about events from your past or present, you are a game changer. More and more people are searching for videos that would entertain them with storytelling. Keep in mind that you have to be entertaining, you have to be able to engage your audience and that your stories have to be very interesting. It is not as much about the topic of your stories as in how you present them. In this niche charisma is everything. However, "storytime" videos are rarely a niche on their own, but many YouTubers use this type of videos to present themselves to the audience and to make themselves approachable. You want your subscribers to know that you are just as human as they are, and they will relate to you. Storytelling videos are often used as a tactic to gain fans loyalty and new subscriptions. Consider using them as part of your chosen niche.

How to Choose Your Niche?

Now that you know why it's important to focus your efforts and your YouTube channel on one niche, you might ask yourself how do you choose the right one? There are certain steps you could take to determine the right niche for you that will turn your YouTube channel into a success. You might have a specific skill you would want to exploit, or a passion which you can monetize through YouTube, but are these really niches that you can exploit? Let's say you play guitar. This is a very saturated area as many people play this particular instrument. What can you do to set yourself apart? This is the most important question you can ask yourself. Maybe beside playing guitar you are also a collector and could show off all the instruments you own and make reviews about them? This is only an example, but there is a way you could determine a niche that is right for you even if you are uncertain what skills you would like to present through your videos.

Start by thinking about broad categories. Maybe you like gaming, which is another very saturated niche. But maybe you particularly enjoy playing retro games. This is a more focused category. Start thinking about your favorite gaming platform, and soon you will come up with a niche that could sound something like "retro games on the sega mega drive". This is a very specific niche, and maybe it even feels limiting. But remember that you are just starting out and your goal is to build up a following. This kind of limit is good for new YouTubers who are looking to gain their first subscribers. Once you produce several videos on this topic and gain a core audience, you might want to expand your niche. Start playing retro games on other platforms, or create different kinds of videos. Make "Top 10 retro games" videos and keep your audience interested but also attract new viewers. Even the most obscure niche has a lot of potential simply because not enough people create that content. It's much easier to sell your content to a starving audience instead of fighting thousands of competitors for the same audience.

However, not everything can be solved with brainstorming. You should always do some research and see what is out there and how successful those niches are. You need to know what people want to see in order to create high quality content to attract them. The research should be done directly on YouTube as this is where you will see the best results. To keep your browser history from influencing your research, you might want to do it in an incognito window. For example, you can directly search for "retro gaming" on YouTube and filter your results by channels. This is still considered a broad category but it will show you what is out there, what other people are doing in this niche and how many views and subscribers they have. You will quickly determine if gameplays have more views than "Top 10" lists, or the other way around. You should do this type of research for all the relevant keywords of a certain category.

Once you choose the general category (retro gaming in our example), and you do your research and have an idea of what's out there, you should return to the goals you set for your channel and decide if you want to educate people, entertain them, or make them laugh. This will narrow down your choices. Maybe you find out that creating informative videos on retro games can pay out more than simply showing the gameplay itself.

After doing all your research and picking your niche, you have to think how to monetize it and if you can keep producing videos on the topic for a sustainable period of time. Make a plan for the future expansion of your niche and extend on what you can do to keep it relevant and interesting for your subscribers. Keep researching even when your channel reaches your set goals. You need to follow the trends and keep yourself in the game. Use tools such as Google Trends to determine the longevity of the topics you are covering in your videos. Also, keep yourself updated on all YouTube and Google marketing tools and algorithm changes and plan your business strategy accordingly.

Chapter 4 - Setting Up Your Account and Channel

You've brainstormed an idea, done some research, and you decided on the niche you want to work in; you are ready to start! You could immediately start making videos and upload them on YouTube, but there is so much more behind a successful channel than shooting videos.

First, you need to set up your account, but you will also have to think about branding your channel. A successful youtuber is more than just a name, or a personality. It is a one-man company, a business, and a brand. You want viewers to recognize your videos when they pop up in their suggestions feed and you want them to be able to search specifically for your channel.

There are many challenges and difficulties on the path to creating a successful channel and we will also discuss how to deal with all of them. Anyone can set up an account on YouTube and create his own channel, but if you want to achieve success, you will have to invest both time and money. You're investing in yourself and in a business, even though sometimes it doesn't feel like it.

Branding Your Channel

People love familiarity and having a routine. This applies to YouTube, and they are more likely to search for the channels they already watched, subscribed to, and enjoyed. Returning viewers are the key just like returning customers matter to every business, and if you want your channel to succeed, you will have to look at it as a business.

To have returning viewers, you have to make it easy for them to recognize you. This is where branding comes in. Branding is important because it's what makes you recognizable, and what makes you stand out from your competition, at least at a first glance. This first glance, the first impression your channel makes is extremely important, just like a book cover draws in a potential reader. People don't know you yet, and they can't decide whether they like your personality just by looking at a single video you created. But the way you present yourself, the way you look, or how your channel in general looks, will leave a very deep impact on viewers.

Your brand identity is the way people perceive you. In this case, you are trying to be likable to YouTube viewers, and make them want to return to your channel. This is why you need to make a good looking channel. Your brand identity needs to express the idea of your channel through your logo, color scheme, typography, thumbnails, your voice, and body language. If you're creating a YouTube channel to promote your already existing business, then you should match the branding of your website with your YouTube channel. After all, the channel is an extension of your business, if not its essence. If you look at some of the most popular YouTube channels, you will notice they are pretty recognizable even without reading the channel name. This is what you want for your channel too. You want people to be able to recognize it instantly and look forward to seeing your new videos.

The first thing you should consider is updating your channel art. Start with a banner because it is the first thing people will see. Decide what colors you will use, as well as the fonts and images. Make them fit the tone of your channel, and correspond to your chosen niche. Although bright colors attract the attention easily, you don't want to use them if your channel has a more serious tone to it. You also want to avoid mixing too many colors, because to a viewer that would be too distracting and confusing. But if you want to start an entertainment channel, you might want to consider the power of flashy and colorful banners. It all depends on your niche and a professional graphic designer might come in handy.

Once you have your banner set up, extend the same branding to your videos and thumbnails. Use the same or similar color scheme, fonts, and overall design. If you use text in your videos to present some data, make sure you use appropriate fonts that fit with the tone of your channel and niche. Thumbnails are extremely important. They are the first thing a viewer sees before even playing a video. If you brand them consistently, people will start recognizing your videos and would click on them just because they are sure of the quality of your channel.

That being said, branding is much more than just the looks of your channel and videos. Although the first impression your viewers are going to have of you is visual, you should strive to extend your brand onto the more technical side of your channel. It is important to understand that people like familiarity. They like consistency, they like their videos to have a beginning, middle, and an end. Because of this, you should consider following a script for your videos. They don't have to be detailed scripts like for TV or radio shows, but at least an outline. Have a good idea in which direction you want to take your audience. That doesn't mean your content will always be the same. You can make it as diverse as you want, but make certain you always follow the same recognizable format.

To discover the format you're going to follow, be creative and feel free to experiment in the beginning. See what works the best for you and your niche. For example, if you have a one on one conversation with your audience, if you're speaking directly to them, consider jump cuts. This way, your viewers won't be distracted, and their attention will be 100% on you and what you're talking about. But if your channel is more visual than auditory, (let's play channel) consider smooth and slow transitions. A good way to decide on your editing style is to research what your competition is doing. This doesn't mean you should copy their style, but get inspired and learn what works and what doesn't.

Finally, you should consider a personal brand even if you don't show your face on the camera often or at all. Sooner or later your viewers will want to learn who is behind this awesome channel they've been following. You need to present yourself in your best light. Keep in mind this is not at all about your looks, although it can play a major role. You need to think about how you express yourself, the way your voice sounds, the words you choose and even your accent. Everything that makes you a person will be judged by your viewers and you should present the best version of yourself. Remember that your viewers are your customers and you should strive to present yourself as you would to your business partners and clients. That doesn't mean you should be strictly professional and serious. Just be yourself or create an entertaining persona if it suits the niche you're focusing on.

What You'll Be Up Against

There are many challenges you will have to overcome as a new content creator. Even when you reach success and you consider yourself in the right place, you will have to deal with some old challenges as well as new ones. The best way to handle them is to anticipate them, be prepared, think two steps ahead, and plan for them. Do not let this discourage you.

Remember that you are not the only one who has to deal with these challenges.

Aside from careful planning, there are support communities out there that will gladly help you, give you advice and nudge you in the right direction. Challenges can be very personal and sometimes feel like they're impossible to face. In those cases you might want to consider hiring outside help. But the majority of the obstacles you will meet as a new YouTuber are pretty common and easy to overcome. Let's examine the most common challenges together. This section will give you an excellent idea about facing future challenges, including unpredictable ones.

Expenses

Starting a YouTube channel that offers value can be a costly endeavour. YouTube is free to all of its users, and anyone can shoot an amateur video on their smartphone and upload it. However, if you want to succeed, you will have to turn to more professional equipment such as dedicated cameras, expensive video editing software, backdrops and lights, and even outside graphic design services. All of this can cost you thousands of dollars if you want a professional production. But remember that expensive gear won't guarantee YouTube success. You should rather concentrate on delivering quality content that offers value to the viewer. The keyword is "value".

Although you should start planning for potential expenses early, you can start small and upgrade as you go. Your viewers will notice the improved quality of your videos, sound, and the production overall and they will appreciate it. But they will stay mainly because your videos are fun to watch, and they deliver exactly what they need.

Don't let yourself be discouraged. Video content creation is a business like any other and you invest into it for your own future. Nowadays, you can buy almost everything you need for less than $1,000 and upgrade as your audience grows. That is a significantly smaller expense than what any other type of business would require.

Search Engine Optimization

YouTube is a search engine on its own, but it also works perfectly with Google because it is part of it. To have your videos rank high on search pages, you need to have an understanding of how SEO works. You need to learn how to optimize the titles of your videos, their descriptions, tags and even comments. SEO is crucial to success and you will often find yourself optimizing your content.

Learning the basics of search engine optimization is a challenge and a requirement if you can't afford to outsource this task. However, there are many tools out there that can help you analyze keywords, trends and help you optimize your channel so it shows up as one of the top search engine results. You can even search for YouTube channels that will teach you how to become a competent SEO specialist.

Competition

YouTube is open to everyone. As a result, sometimes it feels as if your videos are just whispers in a very crowded room. In order to be seen on YouTube you need to stand out. This is one of the biggest challenges you want to address early on in your YouTube career. But the solution to this problem boils down to the goals you set in front of yourself. These goals are a measure of what success is to you. After all, success is a very individual thing. You might consider yourself very successful if you gather more than 10,000 subscribers, or you might strive to gather a million. To beat your competition you will need to offer quality content, value, and choose your niche wisely. If there are many people already doing what you're doing, try to come up with different types of videos and new ways to say what others are already saying. Consider beating your competition with your shining personality or a unique way to present information (such as using cartoons).

In either case, competition can feel overwhelming, but you can learn from it. Study those to succeed and eventually you'll succeed as well.

Time

Being a successful content creator means investing time in your YouTube presence. Ask yourself how often can you post videos, and keep them interesting and of high quality? Do you have a 9 to 5 job that you need to dedicate your time to, or maybe a family that requires your attention. Your subscribers want you to upload your videos regularly. They want to be able to anticipate new content from you. But how frequent you upload content doesn't depend only on your personal time.

The type of content will dictate how often you need to post. For example, tutorials and let's play videos are usually posted three times per week, while educational videos or trivia heavy content would require you to upload a video once a week. Vlogs can be posted daily, weekly, or even monthly, depending on the type of vlog you are doing. There are many factors that will determine how often you need to upload new, engaging content, but most important of all is to set a schedule and stick to it. Be regular and keep your viewers happy.

Earnings

Many people think that successful YouTubers are rich. But success doesn't necessarily equal money as many youtubers are doing it just for fun. There are many ways to monetize your YouTube channel and it can be a real challenge to do it.

The first method that comes to people's minds is advertisement. But the truth is ads don't pay well for the effort you put in your videos. Furthermore, YouTube as a platform will take its cut of the cake from advertisement, leaving you with a smaller share. Ads also pay only if the viewer interacts with them, and doesn't skip them. Nowadays many users skip ads altogether by using free ad blockers. This makes ads a very unpredictable source of income.

Although you shouldn't completely disregard advertisements, there are other ways you can monetize your videos. You can affiliate sales and product promotions, offer various services, engage yourself in larger projects and become a public speaker, or let the fans donate money for your work using platforms like Patreon. Many YouTubers have found success by providing free content without ads and allowing the viewers to support the channel via donations.

Finally, since your youTube channel is a brand and a business, you can always opt to sell your own merchandise to subscribers. If you plan ahead, earnings will come if given enough time.

The Process of Creating Your Channel

Setting up a YouTube account takes only a minute and anyone can do it for free. Even starting a channel is one click away. However, optimizing your YouTube profile to achieve maximum reach is another thing.

In this section you will find a step-by-step guide on how to get your account set up, how to create your own channel, as well as how to optimize it. Don't forget that you need to research before starting your channel and decide on some key points such as: who will be your audience, what is your niche, how successful is your possible competition, and what is the ultimate purpose of your channel.

Step 1: Set up your account.

Because YouTube became part of Google, it doesn't take much more than having a Gmail account to sign up for your YouTube account. You can sign in to YouTube using your smartphone, computer, or tablet. All you have to do is fill in your information. Once your account is created, YouTube will require you to verify it. You will find a code has been sent to your inbox. Use it by following the instructions and your account will be fully set up. It's time to get down to business and launch your channel.

Step 2: Create a channel.

In the top right corner of your screen you will find your profile icon. Click on it, and then choose the "Create a channel" option. This is also where you will have to make your first decision. Do you want a personal account or a business account? The difference between these two options is that with a business account you can set up a different name to your channel and share its management with other people. Once you decide on the type of the channel, give it a unique name.

Step 3: Personalize your channel.

Once you create a new channel, you will notice a new Google account was created with the name of your channel. This is so you can use your brand name to interact with people on YouTube, leave comments on other videos and like/dislike them.

The new Google account comes with its own settings and YouTube history. Through it, you can further customize your channel by adding the description of your channel and inserting links to your main website or other social network platforms. All of this information increases your chances of being found and it increases trust among your viewers.

Step 4: Art

You'll need some digital art to personalize your channel. You can create some by using Photoshop, if you are skilled enough, or you can pay a professional to do it for you. But you could also opt to use free image creators such as Canva or Adobe Spark. They come with YouTube art templates you can use to customize your art to your liking. But keep in mind you should follow the optimal size for the art that YouTube recommends. A single image should not be larger than 2560x1440 pixels. To play it safe, any text you want to include in your art should be within the minimum of 2048x1152 px area to guarantee it won't be cut off when displayed on different devices. Recommended file size is 6MB or smaller.

Step 5: Add a profile picture.

Each channel you create will have a dedicated spot for a profile picture. This is the icon that will show up next to each of your videos, and therefore it's part of your branding strategy.

Take note that the profile picture is limited to 800x800 pixels, so think of something that would look good at small resolution. You can use your logo or the initials of your channel's name. To upload the profile picture, simply hover your mouse over its placement and you should get the option "edit". Click on edit and simply upload your new profile picture.

Step 6: Optimize your channel description

The description space of your channel is limited to 1000 words and you have to be creative and make each one of them count. Remember that description is also indexed by search engines and that is why you should include a relevant selection of keywords and a call to action. The first 100 to 150 words are the most important ones for good SEO because of how search engine algorithms rank them, so make sure to use keywords that accurately describe what your channel is about. However, don't overwhelm the text with them. It should read natural, otherwise Google will lower your ranking due to keyword stuffing.

Step 7: Add relevant links to your channel.

If you click on the "Customize Channel" button on your homepage, and then on the gear icon in the upper-right corner, you will see a Channel Settings lightbox. In order to add links you will have to turn on the "Customize the layout of your channel" option. Now you can go back to your channel's homepage and you will see the "Edit Links" option in the settings menu. Clicking on it, you will get the option to set up links that will be displayed over your cover art. Use this option to make yourself more visible to the search engine and potential viewers.

Step 8: Add a trailer to your channel.

A channel trailer is the best way to introduce yourself and your channel to the viewers. You should create a short, to the point video in which you explain who you are, what your channel is about, and what type of content you have to offer. This trailer should be designed in such a way to attract new subscribers. Make the trailer grab the viewer's attention as soon as it starts, but keep it in the general tone of your channel. These trailers will appear only to the viewers who didn't subscribe yet to your channel, and their purpose is to persuade them you have quality content to offer.

Exploring Your Channel

Congratulations! You just created your first YouTube channel. Now is the time to explore your possibilities. There is a significant difference between the YouTube users who never opt to create their accounts, and the users who have their channels set up. Millions of people use YouTube casually and they never create their own account. But they are at a loss. YouTube allows you to view videos and even share them without ever logging in. But in order to become an active member of the community, you need your own account and channel. This will allow you to upload your own videos, comment on videos, whether they are yours or someone else's, and cut your own corner on the YouTube real estate market. You will also be able to save links for easy retrieval and create your own personalized playlists.

Take some time to explore your account settings, and especially the channel settings to become familiar with the environment. Perform all the steps mentioned above to fully optimize

your channel and prepare yourself to create
your first YouTube video.

Section 3: Creating, Editing, and Posting Videos on YouTube

Chapter 5 - Creating Content

You have an idea for your YouTube channel, you did your research and you know your target audience. You chose your niche, thought about the types of videos you want to make, and set up your own YouTube account. Now the time has finally come to create the content and say "Hello" to the YouTube community.

But how do you do it? You sit in front of your camera and you shoot your first video? Is it really that simple? Well, yes and no. Yes, YouTube is about video content and everyone can upload something and be seen, but not everyone will become successful. Behind a successful youtube channel lies the recognition that the content is so much more than just a video.

First, you will need to establish your own content plan and develop the strategy behind it.

It Depends on Your Niche and How You Strategize

All the great videos out there on YouTube are carefully planned by their creators. Of course, you can make an awesome video without following a strict plan, but could you really keep doing that regularly? You would either have to be very lucky or extremely talented. All the successful YouTube channels strategize their content, and they even go into such details that they write scripts. This planning phase is called pre-production, and if you do it correctly, you will save both time and money.

The first thing you should do is think about who will be watching your video. Who is your audience? But don't fall into a trap thinking you know your video will be viral and everyone would see it sooner or later. You need to understand that your audience is a group of people with different experiences and interests. That group of people will have overlapping interests and you should always strive to create your video content having these overlaps in mind. You need to narrow down your video viewers to a single persona with a set of interests. That way you will be able to create a much more relatable video. Don't strive to please everyone. Think about the age, gender, location, economic status, education level, hobbies, and career of your audience persona.

Once you define your audience, you will have to define the message you are trying to convey to them. There are numerous ways to work within your niche, and you have to make a decision for each video you are making, namely what is going to be its main purpose. Are you going to entertain, educate, or maybe you want to show off your own product? It is incredibly important to tailor a video to carry out a specific message. Planning the message of your content will make it easier to create more fun and engaging videos in the future.

Another thing you should take into consideration when planning your content is the budget. Budget in this sense doesn't necessarily have to mean money you would spend making a video. You can opt for videos that don't require any investment at all. But you should consider the recording equipment you have, and if you need to buy or rent a new camera, light, backdrop, and any other tools. If you have a tight budget, remember that the most important thing in a successful video is the message it's trying to convey. You can be creative and record an interesting video with your smartphone. However, if your niche demands professional visual appeal, you might need to work on getting more adequate equipment.

The script is incredibly important whether you are making a prank video, an educational one, or a simple commercial for your product. If needed, you can write down what you want to say, word for word. But if you are a talented speaker and think you have enough charisma to win over your audience, you could opt to work with a basic outline. This means that planning the script for your videos isn't just writing down the sentences you will be saying. It also involves writing down the visuals you want to use in the video, or when to play music, and when to stop it. Review your script often, and if you're working with more people, listen to their advice and work together on the script.

While writing your script, consider putting your best in the first eight seconds of the video. That is normally how much an average person allows a video to peak his interest. A viewer that clicks on your video in the first place, will click away from it if his attention isn't engaged early on. That doesn't necessarily have to be a bad thing. You don't have to start your video with the most interesting information you have to offer. You can use these first eight seconds to intrigue your viewer, make him want to stay on your video without revealing too much. Think of it as the first paragraph in a new book. It has to grab the audience into a new world. Avoid long and boring introductions in which you would explain the video your viewers are about to see. You should never underestimate your audience's ability to understand your videos.

Determine the length of your videos. The message you want to present to your viewers should determine how long your video presentation should be. There is no need to make it longer than it needs to be. But there is also no need to rush and create short, fast-paced videos so you could save up on time. However, keep in mind that generally, people are not as interested in seeing long videos. Shorter videos have better engagement. This is again connected to the attention span of your audience. Generally the short videos are watched until the end by a large number of viewers. However, if your video is engaging, interesting, and speaks to the right audience, then its length is less important.

Next, you need to plan the location, lighting, outfits you will wear during the recording session, make-up, guests that you will interview, and everything else your video will involve. All these small details are what make the content of your video engaging and interesting, and they should not be taken lightly. But remember, everything needs to be synchronized with your niche and target audience. Don't wear a sports outfit if you're giving a presentation about job interviews. Your audience wouldn't take you seriously. You should also avoid shooting your job interview video guide at a zoo, for instance. The location needs to give a viewer a visual representation of your video's message. Create a simple office setting, or use a neutral backdrop. Planing all these details is part of the creative process. The message you want to spread across YouTube and the internet starts with an idea, not in the camera. Careful planning will help you choose the best possible way of representing yourself, your business, or simply your niche and YouTube channel.

See What the Other YouTubers are Doing

Because YouTube is the second most visited website, right after Google, it holds great potential for many businesses and people who want to succeed. This platform has a space for everyone, from big brands and famous individuals to self-proclaimed YouTubers and influencers. But they didn't succeed by accident, they all used a strategy that helped them be unique. They used data and analysis methods to determine the most effective way to gather subscribers and views. Let's discuss some of the tools you could also use to deduce how well your videos are performing.

YouTube has its own analytics system and it is a great tool for anyone who is just starting their own channel. Known as YouTube Analytics, this tool offers you a very in-depth analysis that will help you understand the performance of your videos. You can also use it to understand your audience and determine its demographics.

You can find this tool in the Studio section of your channel, and you will see that it has many sections and options for you to explore. But it will take you only a short time to find some of the data that will give you an insight into how well your channel is performing. You can see the overall traffic over time and determine when was the point your channel had the most visitors. This is an excellent way of determining at what period your channel is peaking, and you can concentrate on posting in the given time frame. You can also see the view duration of your top-performing videos, and the location of the people who are watching your videos. Swipe to the audience tab and discover the age, gender, and location of your viewers. Sometimes we are simply not reaching the audience we want, and you can make adjustments to your content accordingly.

There are many such tools out there that enable you to see the data behind your channel and analyze it. Some are free, others come with a subscription, but they're equipped with so much more than what YouTube's analytics system has to offer. It is up to you to determine which tools you want, but the general advice is to use at least two and to compare the data you are getting from them. These tools are content marketing tools, and they come with their own integrated YouTube Analytics. Here are a few of them for you to explore: BuzzSumo, Brandwatch, and Social Blade.

Besides analyzing your own channel and videos, you should make an effort to also analyze your competition. By doing so, you will learn a tremendous amount of information that will help you succeed. This is called "competitive benchmarking" and through it, you will see what makes your competition succeed or fail, and you will be able to develop your own strategy around it.

If you notice that your views are dropping, and your main competitor's views are rising, it's time to investigate. See what it is they're doing to attract people and analyze what you're doing wrong. You can even do competitive benchmarking ahead and plan for the future. You don't have to wait for something extraordinary to happen in order to benchmark your competition. Do it before you even start your own YouTube channel just to get a general idea about their success and how you should organize your channel.

There are two ways you can do competitive benchmarking. You can opt to do it manually and look at your competition's views, go through their comments, and learn how they interact with the audience. You can also search for both positive and negative feedback your competition receives to draw your own conclusion on what works and what doesn't. However, if you want more in-depth analytics, you could use some of the aforementioned tools. Unfortunately, YouTube's own analytics tool won't allow you to see your competition's data, but tools such as InfluNex, Rival IQ, and SocialBlade will.

The Win-Win Solution

If you think competition benchmarking is like spying on your fellow YouTubers, be assured that is what everyone is doing and no one will take it as something bad. Learning about other YouTubers, their methods, and successes, as well as failures, will allow you to take your channel to a new level. Content creators are aware of the amount of success they can achieve and that they can prosper if they work together. In the YouTube content-making sphere, this is known as collaboration; collab for short. You should plan in the near future to search for a collab opportunity, because of the many advantages it can bring you.

YouTubers connect with each other through personal outreach, or through apps like Grin. They do this so they could work together and present themselves to each other's audience. There are many YouTubers who create similar content, but while some are famous, others are unknown even though they offer quality content. But YouTube is massive and finding a content creator who caters to all your needs is a difficult task. But if two YouTubers, or more, work together, they can cross-post their collab video and intrigue, engage, and gain a new audience. Sometimes, famous YouTubers will endorse smaller YouTubers by mentioning them in their videos. By introducing this less known channel to their own audience, they can funnel traffic to that channel. Doing collabs is always good for business, but it might not always have the same results.

Collabs need to be planned carefully, and the best thing you could do is to collab with other people who create content in your own niche. This is because if you share the niche, you most certainly attract the same type of audience. If you are doing make-up tutorials, doing a collab with a person who does wildlife content won't bring you many views. But if you collab with a hairstylist, you will reach an audience interested in beauty tips. But sometimes, doing a cross-niche collab can yield success. Let's say you are doing those make-up tutorials because you're a make-up artist. You could collab with a history channel and discuss and demonstrate make-up fashion through various historical periods. This type of cross-niche collab will bring together two audiences and increase traffic to both of your channels.

Sometimes a few smaller YouTube channels can band together and create a strong bond. They can grow into a different, separate channel and attract a huge audience. However, when it comes to collaboration, the trick is in finding the right people to work with. There are millions of YouTubers out there and you should not send the invitation just to anyone. You need to do some research, learn about the top content creators in your niche, and reach out only when you are sure something good can grow out of collaboration. There are forums such as YTTalk, the SocialBlade forum, or TheYouTubeCommunity where you can get to know other content creators and find collab partners.

Once you reached out to other YouTubers and received a positive response, brainstorm together to find the perfect way in which you could collaborate. There are many things you could do together but stick to your own niche. You can interview each other, or simply talk about the interests you share. You can also do a fun video where you challenge each other, or even do a collab intended to raise donations for a noble cause. The options are numerous and they all yield results. Be creative, but also listen to your new collab partner and appreciate their ideas too.

There are other types of collaboration worth mentioning. They wouldn't be with YouTube content creators, but with already established brands that are searching for new ways to advertise themselves. While they are prone to search for famous YouTubers who would do a simple commercial for them, your audience wouldn't appreciate such a collaboration, especially in the beginning. You need to find a way to implement this brand into what you're already doing. Reviews are always a good start, particularly if you already established a level of trust with your audience. Just make sure to stick to your niche and only arrange collaborations with brands that you know will appeal to your audience.

Read This Whenever You're Lost on What to Create Next

There comes a moment in every YouTuber's life when he or she is simply out of ideas what to do next. All artists and crafters have this creative block and everyone deals with it in his own way. However, if you plan ahead, and think of a system that will ensure you never run out of ideas, you won't be in trouble when your channel picks up. This will also help you be consistent in publishing your new videos as you won't waste your precious time brainstorming new ideas.

There are different systems you could use, and the general advice is not to rely on only one. Here are a few things you could do to keep your videos fresh and interesting for your audience:

Read comments and listen to feedback: Your own audience will leave comments on your videos. Sometimes praising and admiring your work, but once in a while, they will leave you suggestions on what you could do next and what they would love to see you do. Take their ideas into serious consideration. Answer your viewers' demands and questions to establish trust and loyalty. You will show that you acknowledge them, you listen, and you cherish their input. Your own viewers will surprise you with some awesome ideas for your next videos!

Do your own research: There are many ways to research new topics. You can read articles, books, or watch other people's videos but you have to confine yourself to your own niche. There is no point in doing research on topics your niche doesn't correspond to. You can even share the story of how you found the information on the topic with your audience. They would love to hear where else they can read or hear about the topics you discuss in your videos.

Get inspired: Inspiration comes in many forms and from many sources. Watch documentaries or movies, even tv shows, read books, and listen to music. All these sources can inspire your next video. Even just simple talk with your friends and family can lead to a new great idea for the next video. Inspiration is all around us, you just have to harvest it. Getting inspired from everyday life is a skill you need to learn. All you have to do is observe everything around you consciously and ask yourself how you can implement what you experience in your videos.

Recycle other YouTubers: Other YouTubers are great sources of inspiration. You should never strive to copy them, but there is no harm if you give your own opinion on the topic already covered by someone else. You can even mention how you were inspired to talk about this topic or to create a video on the given topic by watching another YouTuber. You can even create react videos and argue your point of view. Just make sure to credit them by mentioning their channel, as that could lead to a potential collaboration and spread the news about your channel. Don't be afraid to go to their videos and see the topics they covered even years ago. Some topics are always trendy and you might be able to bring a new perspective.

Here is a list of ideas that can serve you throughout your YouTube career:

- Accept another YouTuber's challenge

- Have an in-depth discussion on the topic belonging to your niche

- Do a reaction video, but keep it closely connected to your niche

- Create a tutorial and show your audience how to do or make something

- Tell a story from your life, people love to connect with YouTubers on a more personal level.

- Include breaking news from your niche

- Go live, and show your audience what you are doing at the moment

- Host a trivia quiz and invite guests and experts from your own niche

- Make first impression videos

- Create unboxing videos if you review a product

- Do a Q&A and answer the questions your audience is asking you

- Include bloopers, and make funny videos of your own recording failures

- Create a "Best of" compilation once in a while involving only the topics of your niche

- Create a comparison video where you compare two similar products

- If you have children, think about including them in some of your videos

- Go outside and interview strangers on the street

- Create a "history of" video where you explore the origins of your chosen topic

- Discuss your favorite movie, music, or book. Again, whatever your niche is, your audience would get a chance to get to know you personally if you include such videos occasionally. Just don't overdo it.

- Include myth-busting videos. Learn about the myths in your niche and show your audience the truth behind them

Constructing Scripts Your Way

The importance of the script can't be underestimated. There are two different ways to make a script: you can opt to write the lines of what you plan to say, or you can simply do an outline of the video which you would follow. The script can be detailed or not. It is there to guide you and make your video production process an easier task. But there are instances where you don't need a script, or where it would even pull you back. For example, you can do an interview with an expert, and prepare all the questions in advance. You can think you are very well prepared for the interview, and your guest will smoothly answer all your questions. But those kinds of interviews can sound posed and feel fake. Prepared questions are always good, but that doesn't mean you need to follow the script in a rigid fashion. Feel free to ask new questions that pop in your mind during the interview, or to construct more questions based on your guests answers, and simply push the conversation in an exciting direction.

Having a script will raise the quality of your videos, make them more cohesive, and let your audience follow your videos naturally.

However, you need to be aware that there are certain rules to writing a script, and in order to have successful videos you should try to follow them. All videos must have an introduction, a middle that will contain most of the actual content and a conclusion. However, it is up to you to balance these three sections.

Introductions can often be unnecessarily long, boring and your audience will lose the attention and move away from your video. Instead, start a video with the most interesting detail of the topic so you grab the viewer's attention, and then move on. Keep it short, to the point and make your message crystal clear. In the discussion section you should go back to the most interesting fact about the given topic and continue building your message there. The point of the message is there, in the main body of your content. As for the conclusion, it serves as the end of your video. Here you can end your video with your own thoughts on the topic, or you can let your guests have a final word (if you choose to host them). Just as the introduction, the conclusion should be kept short and to the point. Try to end your videos with fun facts, a quick summary, or tease your audience with "whats next". Keep them interested and they will want to come back to your channel.

Here are some tips on how to write good scripts:

- Write down the basic elements of the scripts such as the character, ideas, main message, setting of the entire project, and props you would be using.

- Consider your audience, their demographics, maturity level and interests and only then decide on what kind of narrative you want to introduce in your video. Work the idea of your main message around that. Should it contain a dose of humor, be completely serious or maybe you want to present your message through animation?

- See if your viewers had some questions in your previous video that you could answer in your next one. By including your audience and addressing their questions and concerns, you will gain their trust.

- Include emotions, the audience loves to get emotional. You can either express your own passion towards the topic you are discussing, or show emotional footage. Don't forget that happiness is also an emotion and you can use this to make your audience laugh or simply feel satisfied and relaxed.

- Keep the pace of the video steady. Don't rush through certain segments just because you think they are less interesting. Your audience might not agree with you, but that doesn't mean you should drag the video to impossible levels. Keep them flowing naturally and don't limit yourself by strict time limits. Follow the structure and keep your audience engaged.

- Once you are done writing the script, ask someone for their opinion. Use their creativity and work together to improve your script. You can seek a writer's opinion and you can even work with a small test audience to see you your script from the viewer's perspective.

- Review your script several times, and don't be afraid to delete parts of it. Even the best script writers rewrite up to several times. Make sure you are completely satisfied with the script before starting the recording sessions.

Chapter 6 - How to Create or Record Your Videos

Back when YouTube was still a young platform, there were only two kinds of videos: bad and worse. In those days, most people had access to low-quality camcorders and that's about it. Nobody even imagined making professional YouTube videos as a career, so nobody invested in studio equipment and video editing software. The few who did, still struggled making bad videos. Keep in mind that today's cheapest smartphones record better quality videos than most consumer-grade equipment people had access to.

Since those dark times, both hardware and software evolved significantly. Smartphones are more than capable at shooting good-quality videos, professional cameras are quite affordable, studio lights are cheap, and editing software has never been easier to work with. Consumer level video production can be surprisingly good with minimal investment.

That being said, there are no more excuses for creating bad content that includes audio distortions, terrible exposure, and a shaky cam.

All you need to know is the basics of recording and creating a video. So, let's discuss what it takes to create high-quality entertaining YouTube content.

Creating vs. Recording

Video content is valuable and many people prefer it over text. However, not everyone is made to be in front of the camera. Fortunately, to be successful on YouTube you have two choices: you can create your own content or record it. A lot of people who want to get into YouTube content creation falsely assume that they need to show their face and be charismatic to draw in the crowd and be successful. That isn't true. Both video content creation methods are equally viable.

Creating content doesn't necessarily involve any type of recording. You can produce high-quality videos without recording any footage, sounds, or even voice. Everything is generated and put together using software. On the other hand, the recording method implies recording your own video and audio content.

Recording your own content is probably the biggest challenge for most people. You're probably worried about it as well, wondering about your looks, the quality of your voice, your accent if you're not a native English speaker, your demeanor, as well as other human factors. These are things that have to do with you and they're difficult to change. If you aren't made for the camera, you're going to either struggle or have to invest a lot of time and effort teaching yourself how to act. Additionally, there's the hardware factor to consider as well. You would need a camera, or at least a capable smartphone, a tripod, background, studio lights, and all of this costs. It doesn't have to be expensive, but everything piles up. But this doesn't mean you should avoid recording content. It can be extremely rewarding. However, you might want to start off easy by creating content until you learn the ropes and then make the big step towards recording.

There are many ways to create content and make it visually pleasing without ever recording yourself. You can create PowerPoint presentations and source them up with animations, background music, and narration.

Alternatively, if you love writing, you can use intelligent software, like Lumen5, that creates slides automatically after analyzing your text. Afterwards you can add the music, audio, and render the whole project as a video. This method also leads to the creation of the so-called "explainer" videos. This type of content relies on short slide-based presentations to explain a certain topic. It is highly popular nowadays for people that want a quick solution or explanation to a question they have, and there's a lot of programs that provide just that. Adobe Spark is such a program that is available for free and provides you with predefined story structures you can use to create the slide show.

Equipment for Recording Videos

YouTube is highly competitive nowadays with many content creators offering commercial-quality video content. Viewers grew accustomed to quality video and audio production, so you can't get by with a noisy microphone and a cheap camera. However, that doesn't mean you need to go so far as to rent film-making equipment and professional editors. All you really need is the following list of items:

1. **Camera**: This is the most important piece of equipment. While nowadays there are plenty of options, all you need to focus on is having a camera capable of shooting in HD (1080p). Whether it's a

webcam, DSLR, mirrorless camera, or a GoPro, it doesn't really matter. Each type of camera comes with its own set of advantages, but first you need to figure out what you actually need. There's no point in getting the most feature-rich mirrorless camera if you're going to film your face to appear in a tiny window on the side of a gameplay video. That being said, DSLR cameras are the best choice overall because they can shoot HD videos, they're affordable, and they offer you a great deal of control over exposure, depth of field, shutter speed, and ISO.

2. **Microphone**: Audio quality is just as important as video quality. If the audio is bad, the viewer will lose interest and throw you a dislike instead of subscribing to your channel. Your laptop's built-in microphone is not enough, and you should invest in an external one that can eliminate any background noises. But not just any external microphone will meet all your needs. Before you buy one you should learn which type and brand will suit you the best. While the USB microphones are very easy to use, many opt for the Shotgun microphone as the best option.

They pair well with small cameras and will record high quality audio. They can reduce mechanical noise that comes from around the microphone itself and they are capable of capturing clear sounds without picking up ambient noise.

3. **Stabilizer**: In order to make your videos look professional you will have to get rid of the unsteady and shaky footage. It will make your viewers dizzy and less likely to return to your channel. You can opt to use a tripod or a gimbal stabilizer. They are both amazing in stabilizing your videos and photos, but which one you choose depends on the type of videos you're creating. The tripod is a more affordable option but you should invest in a good one as it will provide better stabilization as well as the opportunity to record from different angles. It can even collapse for low angle footage, and it may come with a ball-head which you can turn and shoot from different angles. Gimbal stabilizers are usually used for light cameras such as smartphones or GoPros. They have built-in motors or weights that will balance the camera for

recording much smoother videos. Choose based on your setup and budget.

4. **Lights**: If you plan to record your videos indoors or in low-light light conditions, you should consider purchassing lighting equipment. However, even if you're shooting with plenty of bright light, additional lighting can set the mood of your video, or break the sharp shadows often created by hard natural light. There are various types of lighting equipment and you should choose according to your needs. A softbox is good to start with because it softens the natural light coming through the window. Umbrella lights will also create soft light, but you will have more control over them as they're easy to move around as needed. As for ring lights, they're ideal if you record yourself indoors. It emits light around the subject isolating it and making it the centre of viewers attention. Finally, if the lighting conditions are bad where you're filming, you should purchase one or two studio lights to act as the primary source of light.

5. **Video Editing Software**: Now that you have all the equipment you need to

record your first video, you will also need a little extra to push the quality of the video through post-production and shape it into the final, presentable product. Video editing software will help you make amazing videos by allowing you to control their length, effects, filters, insert text, animations, edit sound, add music, and so much more. You will discover most of your creativity in post-production. There are many programs to choose from, such as Adobe Premiere and Corel VideoStudio, but most of them come with a subscription fee atached. If you need a basic editor, you can get away with YouTube's YouTube Studio but it comes with limited options. Try finding one which will suit all your needs and you will have no trouble learning how to use it. Most of them have the same features and the only major difference lies in the interface.

Guide for Recording Videos

Bad videos stick out like a sore thumb and viewers won't return to your channel if you fail to deliver quality. When it comes to good videos, it is hard to pinpoint a single element that makes them good. Good videos are attractive, informative and they make us feel a certain emotion. YouTube experts and seasoned content creators always speak about the importance of story and that a video without one is considered bad even if it is technically executed to perfection. However, that doesn't mean you should ignore the technical aspect. Your story won't be interesting enough if your video makes the viewers feel dizzy due to shaky camera work. Aside from story, the video shot with a steady camera, under good lighting conditions and with top-quality audio, will attract more viewers. People are attracted to good visuals. A good video is just that, a story, but you want to offer the best. The best video is the combination of the two factors: story and technical execution.

In order to get the best out of your storytelling abilities, as well as out of your recording equipment, here are some tips for shooting professional YouTube videos:

1. When you shoot your own video you have full control over the process. To execute it properly, you should make a storyboard and include the illustrations of the scenes you are planning to shoot. The storyboard will be your guide during

the shooting but it will also help you finalize your video in post-production. A storyboard should also contain information such as the schedule of shooting, venue, the equipment needed, and the perfect time of the day for a certain scene. It's similar to a script, but it allows you to visualize your plan of action so that you can implement it step by step.

2. No matter if you use your smartphone, GoPro, mirrorless or DSLR camera, remember to shoot horizontally. Vertical or portrait footage is a clear sign of amature content. Horizontal, or landscape footage will play without problems on all devices, while vertical looks ok only on phones.

3. Mind the location of your videos and what you can use for the background. Make an effort to choose a simple background which will not distract the viewers' attention. There should be no action in the background, and if possible, use neutral colors. Many people use a simple wall, some kind of backdrop, or a green screen and these are all good solutions. Your subject should always be

several feet away from the background. This separates the subject better and draws the viewer's eye to focus on it.

4. Improve the composition of your scenes. Even if you have an awesome story to tell, and the high-end equipment to record it, your video won't turn out professionally if your composition and framing are bad. You should always strive to arrange all the visual elements in the scene in a way to tell a story. This will also make the scene aesthetically pleasing and enjoyable to watch. One of the basic composition rules for videographers is the **Rule of Thirds**. You should place your main subject's head slightly above the centre of the frame, and leave plenty of room on the side which the subject is facing. If you're doing close-ups, and if you have to cut off your subject, do it from the top.

5. Use manual focus on your stand-alone cameras or exposure-focus lock on your smartphone. This will allow you to set focus using your own eyes instead of relying on the camera. Autofocus is very handy, but it will often bring the subject in and out of focus if there is movement

in the scene or the light isn't constant. Manual focus will also help you to have control over the depth of field and if used properly, manual focus will help you tell a story.

6. Expose all your scenes evenly and adjust the white balance on all your devices, if you're using multiple cameras to record. This way you will avoid having different exposure, light color and temperature.

7. Shoot with editing and post-processing in mind. This means that while shooting you should keep editing in mind and maybe take a scene from different angles, make safety shots, and plan for the cuts and transitions. This will save you a lot of time in the editing software, and you will have different material to choose from and not settle for the bad scenes just because you have no other. It will also save you from re-shooting if something goes wrong.

8. If you're shooting with your smartphone, avoid the front camera. Use only the back one. Front cameras are usually of lower quality and will produce worse video and audio.

9. Clean your lens. No matter if you record with a camera or smartphone, lenses will often gather dust and dirt which can be seen in the final product or cause focusing issues. You want your videos to be clean and focused on your subject. A speck of dust can distract the viewer or, if large enough, ruin the whole video by covering up a part of your main subject.

10. If you don't have a stabilizer, hold your camera or smartphone with both of your hands, close to your body and if possible, lean against a wall or a tree. This will stabilize you, and in return stabilize the camera. This method is not as effective as having a tripod, but it will reduce the shaking. Besides, modern smartphones and cameras come with the lenses equipped with image stabilizers (not nearly as good as actual stabilizers). However, you should always strive to give it as much stability as possible.

11. Avoid using zoom, especially on your smartphone. Zoom tends to create unstable scenes because the movement it captures is difficult to control. Smartphones use digital zoom instead of optic zoom and the result is digital noise

which will make your videos look unprofessional.

Creating Videos without Recording

There is a reason why YouTube named its users "content creators" rather than "video makers". Not everything posted on YouTube is recorded, and there is no rule that says video must be included. If you ever used YouTube to listen to music, you are certainly familiar with the fact that musicians often use their album cover to display as a steady image instead of a video, while the song is playing. This is not only cutting the costs of video production, but it also allows listeners to focus on the audio rather than video. There are many reasons why some YouTubers prefer to not use cameras and create their content in different ways. Maybe they're shy and don't like being in front of the camera, or their talents lie in storytelling rather than visual presentation. If you are among the people who want to explore alternative ways of creating content for YouTube, without using the camera, here are a few popular methods:

1. **Use artificial intelligence.** Yes, AI can make videos for you from scratch

using tools like Vedia AI and Softcube. Technology has come a long way. All you have to do is type what you want your video to be about. Enter the text and the AI will choose the appropriate royalty free images and videos, as well as speech, music and sounds. AI will also use automated editing tools and create a finished product. However, keep in mind that there is no AI platform which is fully automated. You will still have plenty of control over the video being created.

2. **Opt for Screencast.** If you have no time to record and edit videos, but you need content for your YouTube channel, live streaming is always a good option. You can stream directly what you're doing on your computer. It can be gameplay, or you could show off your photography editing skills. You're a digital artist? Show how you draw and what tools you're using. Teach people how to create short and funny animations. Screencasts can even be live streamed, and YouTube will record it for you so you can share it at later times. That being said, this option can be applied only in certain niches, so keep that in mind.

3. **Create a PowerPoint video.** Yes, PowerPoint allows you to export videos. But making a video using this program can be time-consuming and the results might not be as you would expect. However, it is still a good way to create content without using a camera. You can record only a voiceover or you can use AI to read the prepared text that would accompany the video. Many tutorials are created this way.

4. **Create an animated video.** Animation will allow you to be creative and you'll have full control over your video. You don't have to be an artist or professional animator to create this type of videos nowadays. There are online services that will allow you to create animation videos using only your own sketches. The sketch will guide the program how to create a polished animation as an end result. However, for the high-quality animations you should still invest in a skilled artist.

5. **Use stock images to create a video.** You can use video editing techniques to create an interesting video out of still images. This type of content solution is

best suited for informative videos such as news, history facts, short commercials, and various tutorials. To keep the video interesting you can try zooming in and out, panning, transitioning and different effects and filters which will make your end product aesthetically pleasing.

6. **Use stock videos.** Just as you have stock images at your disposal, you have stock videos and clips too. By carefully choosing stock videos you can create an awesome video which will successfully convey the message, tell a story and evoke an emotion in your viewers.

7. **Repurpose existing videos.** If you have a rich YouTube channel with plenty of content but no time to record a new video, you can recycle your old content. Simply repurpose segments of different videos and be creative with the material you already have. Maybe you saved some unused material from previous shootings and now you can use them to create new content for your channel.

In the end, you can combine all of these methods for non-recorded content. You can combine animation with still images, or screencast. The possibilities go as far as your imagination can carry you. Be creative and come up with your own ways to create YouTube content without using a camera.

Chapter 7 - Editing Videos Like a Pro

Editing videos is a time-consuming process, but a necessary one. Be prepared to learn various tools and even when you think you know everything, you might surprise yourself by discovering new features and ideas.

To edit your own videos you will have to learn how to use editing software, but you will also have to learn some fundamental techniques experienced film makers have been using for decades. This chapter will teach you how to finish your videos and turn them into presentable final products. Start editing like a pro!

The Makings of a Great Video

The editing stage of video creating is usually referred to as post-production. No matter how tedious this step feels like, nobody should skip it. Otherwise, your product would be a pile of mess and unpresentable to the audience. Video editing and post-production in general, are there to put all of the aspects of the video together. It will give your video a perfect flow. With cuts, pacing, and sound effects, your video will become a perfect piece, enjoyable to watch because the narration and pacing are consistent.

Video editing involves blending images and sounds together in perfect harmony. It is the editing that will emotionally connect the viewers to your video. But be aware, bad editing can harm your videos even more than an unedited one. That's precisely why it is important to master the video editing skills on your own. Even if you intend to use a professional editor, you should know the fundamentals of editing otherwise you may end up conveying the wrong message.

Before you dive into editing, you should learn the file formats, resolutions, and conversions you will work with. Knowing these will help you make editing decisions and produce amazing final videos. Modern editing programs are able to handle these on their own, but you still need to know your options.

Videos are large files, and in order to handle them more easily you will have to compress them. Video editing software is able to use certain calculations to squeeze high-quality video and sound into the smallest possible file size. Without compression, your videos can be up to 50 times larger than the final product.

The part of software which handles the compression is called a codec. There are different types of codecs and if your video editing software uses, for example, codec A, you won't be able to watch that video on a device which supports only codec B. However, YouTube supports the most common ones.

Some of the popular codecs out there are: Apple ProRes. Windows Media (WMV), Digital Video (DV) and MPEG-4. Codecs will compress your videos and together with the additional information (video title, synchronization, subtitles) will save them as a certain file format. The file format can be Flash Video (.flv), QuickTime (.mov), Windows Media (.avi), MP4 (.mp4) or MPEG (.mpg). When a video is saved in one of these file formats, it can be played with different kinds of codecs. Modern editing programs can work with any of these file formats. However, there are some exotic file formats and if you encounter them there is a possibility you will have to convert them to a format your editing software can recognize. There are video conversion programs out there, but your main editing program might already have one integrated.

Beside file formats and codecs there are other video editing terms you will have to familiarize yourself with. Here you can learn the meaning of the most commonly used ones:

- **Aspect Ratio**: is the relation between the height and width of your videos. The dimensions are expressed through aspect ratio, and the most common ones out there are: 4:3, 16:9, 1.85:1. YouTube is capable of changing the aspect ratio of your videos based on the device a person is using to play it. However, avoid adding borders or vignettes to your videos as they can confuse YouTube's algorithm into displaying a wrong aspect ratio.
- **B-roll**: is a supplemental footage that is used to make the transition between the scenes smoother. For example, an additional scene can make the viewers' eyes transition smoothly to different points of view. B-rolls are commonly used in movies, news, and interviews.
- **Bit Rate (Data Rate)**: is the amount of data used in each second of your video. It is measured in kilobits per second

(kbps), and they can be constant throughout the video or they can change.

- **Color Temperature**: refers only to the visible light in the video and it can range from cool to warm. This is because cooler colors have a bluish tint, while the warm ones are closer to orange and red. The color temperature is measured in Kelvins.

- **Compositing**: is a process of combining the images using the video editing software. Graphical elements can also be added to the video and this type of compositing will produce a different kind of a single screen image.

- **Crop Factor**: is a number that represents the ratio of your cameras sensor's imaging area to that of a full frame sensor. It is typically presented in numbers between 1.3 and 2.0.

- **Frame Rate**: is the video information captured by the camera's sensor in 1 second. The frame rate is represented through frames per second and the common ones are: 24, 25, 29.97, 30, 50, 60. Shooting at 60 FPS offers the smoothest experience, but 30 FPS is still commonly used.

- **J-cut**: refers to the point where the audio of the next scene precedes the video. They are used creatively to stir emotion in viewers before they are even able to see the next scene. Don't confuse J-cuts with Jump-cuts, those are two different things.
- **Jump-cuts**: are abrupt changes between the scenes. They can make your videos look unprofessional if used wrong and you should avoid using too many of them.
- **L-cut**: is the opposite of the J-cut. The audio of the first scene continues into the next scene.
- **Resolution**: is the number of horizontal and vertical pixels in your video. But sometimes, the resolution is determined only by displaying the number of the vertical pixels (480p, 720p, and 1080p).

These are just some of the video editing terms you should remember. There are more and in time you will learn them. The best way to learn video editing is to simply dive into it and experiment. You can make a short test video and practice on it. You'll learn a lot more that way and a lot quicker. Once you feel confident enough, you can start creating videos for your YouTube channel.

Using Video Editing Tools

Video editing involves using your raw footage to create a final video product out of it. However, you can't turn bad footage into a high-quality production. There's no magic way around it. You should strive to obtain good footage from the start and improve it through editing. Fortunately, for most of the viewers, the quality of the video comes from its ability to tell a story. It's not about the pixel count, but about the message you are trying to send, and about the way you're doing it. Video editing will help you create the best possible way of conveying your message. There are various video editing programs, some are free, others are expensive, and they all come with their own unique features. It is quite possible you will end up using more than one editing software to create amazing videos. But nobody can tell you what to choose and what to stick to. It depends on your budget, technical requirements, and willingness to learn. Here are some ideas of what is out there so that you can find what suits your needs.

VSDC is a free program for editing and it is a good choice for beginners. The program comes with options such as blend overlays, as well as mask and key options. It will allow you to control the speed of your videos as well as transition filters. Some users claim this program is not user-friendly, but the fact it's free still makes it a solid choice for a beginner to practice the basics.

iMovie is another free editing tool for beginners, but only for Mac users. This program offers you various templates that enable you to create quick finished footage. It also has a variety of animated titles and transitions that will give an extra spark to your video without any effort. However, iMovies lacks elaborate options and while it is good for quick clip cutting and putting together different scenes, it will not make an elaborate, high-quality video. That being said, it's still a great option for a beginner.

EaseUS Video Editor is a powerful and easy to use platform which will allow you to create beautiful end-product videos without much technical knowledge. It is beginner friendly, and it comes with over 50 special effects and transitions you can use. It will also teach you how to use more elaborate editing components such as hue and saturation, speed, multiple audio tracks, and much more. It also allows voice-over recording without ever leaving the program.

Adobe Premiere Pro is an advanced editing program and lots of people choose it as their only editing program. You will need some time to learn how to best use this program because of a myriad of options, but once you get the hang of it, your video editing process will become very simple. Furthermore, Adobe Premiere Pro has some automatic features as well that speed up the process. Use this software once you familiarize yourself with the basics, otherwise you may feel overwhelmed.

PowerDirector comes for a price, but it's worth it. This program is extremely user friendly and it has advanced video editing options such as 360-degree footage, motion tracking, and keyframing. PowerDirector will allow you to create complex videos for any niche.

Adobe After Effects is probably one of the most powerful editing programs out there. It is a complex software that will allow you to integrate animations with your videos and will allow you the usage of third party plugins. It is meant for experts but anyone can learn how to use it. The possibilities with Adobe After Effects are limitless. If you can imagine it, this program can do it. However, the learning curve for this program can be steap. There are various tutorials out there, and a supportive community of users that can make the learning process more enjoyable.

The Actual Process of Video Editing

Each video editor has his own workflow and will do the job in his own, unique way. In time, you will find your own way of editing and you will be able to add your own signature to the videos you're making. However, there are six basic steps you could follow and make the job much easier.

Video editing is done in stages, and aside from knowledge, you need to know how to organize your workflow for maximum efficiency. Each step of the video editing process needs to build upon what was accomplished in the previous stage. This way your video editing process will not only be efficient, but the end result will be a coherent video.

The Preview

This stage is part of pre-production and post-production as well. Start by visualizing what you want your end result to be. Write down the ideas and shoot accordingly. Then you can start reviewing the material you got and discard unusable clips. This way you will save time by not importing unusable scenes into the video editing program in the first place. If you're missing some material, now is the best time to re-shoot.

Planing

With your end goal in mind, plan the construction of your video. Which footage needs to be in each segment of the video. Plan the beginning, the middle, and the end of your video and choose the clips you want to include in these parts of the video. Write down all the ideas you have and elaborate them on paper before you import your clips to the editing program. Planning ahead of time will save you from a lot of frustration and wasted effort.

The Rough Cut

At this stage you should prepare your images and clips in the right order. You should also choose the sound effects and music, and include them in the video. The rough cut will give you an idea how various clips and images work together to make the final video. If something works differently than what you imagine, it's not too late to change the concept, or even reshoot.

Scene Editing

Once you're satisfied with your rough cut, it's time to start working on the details. You can cut your clips to the exact point where you want them to start and end. You will now decide on the type of the transition between the scenes and clips, but don't forget to be consistent. If you use multiple transition types your viewers can get confused and have trouble following the flow of your videos.

Effects

Once your overall cut is ready, it's time for the most fun part of post-production: adding the special effects. Keep in mind that simple is almost always better. You are not a Hollywood movie editor playing with CGI (unless that is your niche and specialty). This is the time to add the titles, music, sound effects, and other fine details to your video. Maybe you opt to use slow-motion, color filters or time lapse footage. Keep in mind that the effects need to help you tell the story. Avoid unnecessary flashy effects that will distract the viewer.

Rendering

The final stage of the video editing process is choosing the file format and saving your video to upload it on YouTube. There are different rendering requirements for each file format. The best option is to choose the format which matches the frame size and frame rate of your video. Many editing programs can make this process easy for you as they offer different templates for different streaming platforms. YouTube is always among them. Depending on the length of your video, its complexity as well as the power of your computer's processor, rendering time can vary.

How to Add Music

Music is a really important element that enhances your videos. It speaks to the viewers on a different level. Together, the auditory and visual stimulants complete the message you're trying to communicate to your audience. Music is often used to add the emotional depth to your videos. We all know watching videos without any music feels really strange.

The first thing you need to do when choosing music is making sure it's not under copyright. Now, you might think that means you will need to create your own music. But this is not true. You have options. There are various stock sites which can sell you or offer you for free, music samples and audio tracks. Once you download it, you receive the rights to use it for your videos. They work just like stock images and videos.

The video editing software of your choice probably has an awesome tool which will help you implement the audio. But there are also separate tools that can do this job for you. They all work similarly so you will have to take into consideration the following aspects: your budget, the interface, input formats, and audio control. The tools can also be online or offline. Some of the most popular online tools are Pixico, Kapwing, MP3 Care, Animoto, and of course YouTube Studio. Among these, YouTube Studio is probably the simplest to use. All you have to do is choose the music which is already uploaded to YouTube. Once you start uploading your video, YouTube Studio will start automatically adding your chosen music to it, and it will synchronize the two components.

Other online tools are more complex and they will give you more control of the audio settings. However, they usually come with a price.

If you want to use offline tools to add the music to your video instead, you can opt for any of the video editing programs we explored earlier. They come with this option, but be aware they support only certain music file types. Furthermore, offline video editing programs are usually more sophisticated and will give you many options. However, they can be too confusing and not as user-friendly as tools like YouTube Studio. If you're a beginner, you might stick to one of the online tools and focus on building up your video editing skills first.

Tricks to the Trade

Post-processing is mostly about creativity and less about technical knowledge. However, that doesn't mean you can go creating awesome edits without any technical knowledge. This is why it's important to choose the right software, the one you find easier to use, and that can perform all the actions you need. Consider the interface, the available features and its usability and find the one you will enjoy using the most. The latest and the most advanced video editing program is not always the best choice because it can be less suitable to your own editing style. If you're just starting out, using tools that are industry-standard will most likely push you away from the content-creation process.

Furthermore, you need to pair video editing software with a good computer. It doesn't really matter what you choose, but it has to be fast enough to be able to render your videos in due time. Video files are huge and your computer also needs to be able to offer you a smooth workflow in video editing software. Choose a good processor with a high core count, invest in a fast storage device (SSD), and increase your computer's memory (RAM).

Once you have a powerful computer that can render quickly and a good video editing software, it's time to be creative. Instead of impressing your audience with flashy animation and special effects, always strive to edit your videos for the story you're trying to tell. Your video has to be aesthetically pleasing but also to evoke the right emotion from your audience. Select appropriate music that matches your video and make sure it sets the right mood. You don't want a love ballad in your compilation of funny animal videos. It simply doesn't make sense. You can also choose to add texts and graphics to your videos which would explain the details and facts about your topic. However, this greatly depends on the type of the videos you're creating.

Here are some video editing tips and tricks you can use to make your videos look more professional:

- **Montage**: This technique places the accent on the passage of time. Quick cuts are put together to give a context to the story. It is mostly used to show how a character changed over a certain period of time. Think about the Rocky Balboa exercising scenes in the movie "Rocky".

- **Cross Dissolve**: This is another technique that can be used to signal the passage of time, but it can also be used in many different ways. For example, you can use it to show parallel storylines which are happening at the same time.

- **Fade in/out**: Again, we have a technique used to present the passage of time. One scene is fading out while the new one is fading in. This technique is often used to fast forward in time without too much explanation or to change locations. It is also used to show the transition from day to night and vice versa.

- **Cross Cuts**: Also known as parallel editing, this technique is about switching between two scenes happening at the same time but in different places. Cross-cuts are often used to add tension to the video, expectation and uncertainty. But they are used in other ways too, for example to amplify emotion.

- **Pull focus**: This trick will help the audience focus on the text or a title, while the scene is running in the background out of focus. This way the background is blurred, but the letters are sharp and easy to read.

Chapter 8: You Don't Just Upload a Video

You might think your video is ready for upload once you're done editing it, and although there is no rule which would prevent you from doing so, you should think about several factors. Remember that careful planning is the key to YouTube success, so you will have to include the video details, thumbnails, and your upload schedule in the initial planning. In this chapter, you will learn the importance of having a video schedule and everything you need to know about the details that accompany your video. At the end of this section, you will find a detailed guide on how to upload your first video to YouTube.

The Video Details

Many people think once they finish editing the video and they upload it to YouTube, it's out there, ready to be seen, and that's that.. However, that's not quite how it works. Any piece of content on the internet needs to be properly described in order to be discovered. This description comes in three parts: the title, description, and tags. Together they are referred to as the metadata of the video and they help your viewers find your video. They also notify YouTube about the content of your video and how to categorize it.

Titles are a big part of the YouTube ranking algorithm, but they are also what your viewers will most likely search for. This is why you need to think about the audience's possible choice of words before creating the title for your video. These keywords need to accurately describe your video and they have to make sense when put together. You can't simply throw in all the words that are related to the content of your video. For example, If you made a video of your dog barking at a postman, you can't just title it "barking, postman, dog, at". Put it in order to make sense for the viewer as well as the algorithm, and type something like "a dog barks at a postman". Or for even better searchability, add more details: "funny German Shepherd dog barking at postman". This way your title will capture the attention of those who search for funny videos, dog lovers, and those who exclusively search for German Shepherd videos.

Avoid using personal names in video titles unless the video is about a well-known person. As time passes, some titles get less and less traffic. You should occasionally review them and update them with new, high-traffic words. Avoid clickbait and misleading titles, this will greatly influence your ranking. Keep the titles under 70 characters if possible, and put non-essential details such as the number of the episode or brand name at the end of the title.

Next, we have the description. The description is a longer section of metadata and it will allow you to use as many keywords as you want. You can use up to 5,000 characters to accurately describe what your video is all about. It is highly desirable to use all of them. If you put well-researched keywords in the video's description, it would be a huge boost to visibility. YouTube will accurately index and rank your video, making it available to a wider audience. The YouTube description should be well planned because the search page will display only the first 120 characters. This doesn't influence the indexing itself, but rather how the audience perceives your video. Dedicate those first 120 characters to carefully selected words to grab the viewer's attention and make them want to watch the video.

There are many practices when it comes to writing a good description. Aside from using carefully chosen keywords, you might want to add time codes (timestamps). This will help your viewers jump to the parts of your video that are of interest to them. But do this only if your video is very long. You can also add links to your description section. They can lead to your website, your profiles on other social networks, or your other YouTube channels. Credit the people who worked with you on the video, and also credit the music and images that are not yours, but you used them to create your video. At the very end of the description, you may want to call the viewers to subscribe to your channel or direct them to other videos you created on a related topic.

Finally, you have to pay attention to tags. The tags are what will help your video get discovered by people who search a certain keyword in the search bar or even search engines such as Google. The better tags you chose, the higher your video will be ranked on the search results page. However, you must understand that search engines don't tolerate using irrelevant tags. In fact, if you use tags that you know are generating high traffic, but are not related to your video, you will eventually be penalized by the algorithm. Research the relevant keywords, place the most important ones first, and the least important ones last. Youtube has three different types of tags: specific, compound, and generic. Each one of them has a different purpose and you should always treat them separately. Only that way you will get the best results and attract the audience to your channel.

The specific tags are keyword-oriented and they notify YouTube about the content of your video. Without them, YouTube won't know how to categorize your video or how to rank it. Once you start typing these keywords, YouTube will immediately recognize the content of your video and it will try to suggest some of the keywords that are related, which should be helpful.

The compound tags are tags that use more than one word. Some users even tag the whole title of their video. But YouTube allows only 500 characters to be used as compound tags and if you want to use your title as a tag, you will have to keep it short. When writing compound tags avoid using prepositions such as: or, as, and, if, etc. Not only will you save room for more important words, but YouTube also ignores prepositions completely when it comes to ranking videos.

Last but not least, we have the generic tags, which are one or two-word descriptions of your entire video. They should be used in all of your videos, across your entire channel. Because they are repeating and constant, these tags are very important, so don't forget to include them when you upload each new video.

Creating YouTube Thumbnails

Thumbnails are like billboards for your videos. They instantly tell the viewer that the video is interesting. This is why they are extremely important, and a well-designed Thumbnail can attract the attention of a new audience for your channel. You can always opt to simply use a freeze-frame to tell your viewers what your video is about, but this usually doesn't attract much traffic. You need to make it engaging!

The thumbnail is a small, clickable snapshot and it is as important as your video's title. Because YouTube's ranking system also considers how many clicks your video generates in the first hour since the upload, you want your thumbnail to attract the audience to actually click.

However, Keep in mind it isn't enough to have just a flashy thumbnail. YouTube actually registers for how long a viewer watched your videos. If he just clicked and immediately left because your video wasn't interesting, YouTube will take note of it, and rank your video lower. This is why it is important to use a thumbnail to attract the right kind of audience. Your thumbnails should always portray what your videos are about. This way they will attract only the audience that will stay and watch your content until the end.

More than 90% of content creators have custom-made thumbnails. This is because thumbnails are the first thing a viewer will see when he searches for a certain video. The thumbnail should always contain key information about your video and go well with the title. The two go hand in hand to inform the audience that the video is worth watching. Choose an image that looks great in large and small format and is eye-caching and appropriate for the audience you want to attract. You can opt to use text in the thumbnail, but make it short and easy to read. Use a large font that is clear and concise. Thumbnails show up in different sizes on YouTube and on external websites that contain links to your videos. Therefore, it's important to create a thumbnail that will look good in different sizes and on different devices.

Using misleading or clickbait thumbnails and titles is a sign of sensationalism and is off-putting to the audience. Your viewers might get offended or annoyed by your misleading thumbnails and will most likely not recommend your video to others. Your goal is to grow a loyal audience and once you become recognizable, include your brand in the thumbnail. This way the audience will look forward to seeing the new videos you created. Avoid deceiving your viewers and misrepresenting your video. Keep it simple and to the point. Refrain from using offensive language or images. Never promote violence or sex through images, text, or the video itself. It will not only discourage the viewers from clicking on your video, but you will also lose a chance to monetize your content. Many advertisers choose carefully with whom they want to be associated, and they exclude the YouTubers who promote sex and violence. Finally, you should also avoid using ALL CAPS letters in thumbnails and in your video titles. Most people find it off-putting.

Once you have your thumbnail set, you can use YouTube Analytics to see how they perform. Observe what a viewer does once he clicks on the video. You will easily come to the conclusion whether your thumbnails and title work well enough to attract the desired audience. If you find they don't, you can make the necessary changes easily. There are plenty of free online YouTube thumbnail creators, and they will even give you a variety of templates to choose from. But you can always upload your own photo, add the text you want, or the desired clip art. You can even change the background and the color of the thumbnail. Once you are done with the creative process, all you have to do is download the finished product to your device, so you can use it on YouTube. It is that easy to make a thumbnail. Here is a shortlist of thumbnail makers you can try for free:

1. **Canva**: It has more than 2 million images in its database, hundreds of fonts, and it will allow you to customize the background, colors, and text however you want.

2. **Adobe Spark**: It comes with built-in themes you can use. All of them come with their own color choices, fonts, and layouts, and they are already designed to catch the eye of potential viewers.

3. **Crello**: This service will allow you to quickly blend images, text, designs, and objects. It's an easy-to-use program that

will allow you to explore your own creativity.

4. **Picmaker**: Picmaker comes with a huge database of stickers, photos, backgrounds, text, icons, and much more. But it will also allow you to erase the existing background on some of the images, so you can use them as creatively as you want.

5. **Snapp**a: This program has a big assortment of templates, as well as customizable text, images, and objects that you can use to create thumbnails for your videos. The simple drag and drop functionality will allow you to do it fast even if you are not an expert.

Setting an Upload Schedule

In previous sections, we mentioned that scheduling the publishing of your videos is very important. It is one of the best ways of growing your audience and subscriber base. But being regular will also keep your existing subscribers interested as they will know when to look forward to your content. A schedule will also keep you disciplined and you will look forward to creating the content for your YouTube channel. It is often difficult for some creative people to stick to a schedule because they are inspired in the moment and inspiration might not visit them for months. However, with YouTube, it is unlikely to grow a substantial follower base and become successful if you're posting your content on the spur of the moment. It is essential that you make great content that you are passionate about, but remember that it isn't the only thing that will bring you success.

Even if you are not used to making schedules and organizing your creativity, you can still do it. It is a matter of discipline. Here is what you can do to get into the routine:

1. Be specific! Don't simply say to yourself "I'm gonna post two times a week". That is not enough. You have to decide on a specific day and set even the specific time frame when you will post your new content. Let's say you set your posting time to be each Wednesday at 2 PM. Your viewers will know exactly when to log in and see your new content. Remember how we said the first hour is very important for your video to get ranked? Well, this is how you do it. Your fans will watch your video immediately, allowing

your video to rank higher and attract new audiences.

2. Make your posting schedule public. You can post it in the description of your channel, intro video, or on your banner. The audience will want to see your schedule and anticipate your new content. It will also allow your new subscribers to get to know your routine.

3. Remember that uploading a video takes time. You also have to dedicate time to writing the description, title, and creating the thumbnails. It might be easier if you prepare yourself in advance. Write down everything you need to have it ready on the day of upload.

4. Resist posting ahead of your schedule. It might happen that you feel extra creative, and you make two videos instead of one. Resist posting them both at the same time, or one immediately after the other. Bank your extra video and have it ready for the next scheduled publishing period. This way you will always have a video ready to post, even when you don't feel creative enough to create new content.

If you have a verified YouTube channel, and by this point, you should, YouTube will allow you access to a neat feature called "scheduling". This feature will allow you to upload a video ahead of time, but publish it only on the specific date and time you set. Uploading and publishing used to be synonyms in the world of YouTube, but not anymore. However, to use this feature you will have to go through a bit of effort on setting it up. Make sure your video status settings are not set to Public, Unlisted or Private. They should be set to Scheduled. Once you do this, you will have to choose your date and time of publishing the video. YouTube will need you to confirm your settings through email. Once everything is set up, you can relax and YouTube will automatically publish your content on the date and time you chose. You might as well be on a vacation and not worry about your schedule or channel!

Yet another trick to successfully scheduled YouTube videos is determining the perfect day and time of publishing. You can do this by checking YouTube Analytics and determining on what day and at what time your videos are most viewed. This will highly depend on your audience demographic. If you want to succeed worldwide, YouTube suggests posting on Thursdays and Fridays between 12 and 3 PM.

This is because, on those days, YouTube itself has the most visitors. Following the same data, you can determine the worst days for publishing your content and avoid those days.

How to Upload Your Videos

Now that you know how to fill in your video's details, add metadata, tags, a proper title, and a thumbnail that will attract your audience, it is time to learn how to upload the video. You can either opt to use YouTube's application or do it via your web browser. There is not much difference between these two options and most of the steps are the same. But this chapter will teach you how to do it properly no matter what device you are using.

Uploading a video through the web browser:

1. Using your favorite web browser navigate to YouTube.

2. Log in if needed.

3. On the top of the screen, you will find the "create a video" button, click it. In the drop-down menu find the option "upload video" and select it.

4. YouTube will take you to the upload page where you will find "select files to upload". Choose the status of your video: "Public, Private, Unlisted or Scheduled". Public videos can be seen by anyone. Private means only you have access to it. An unlisted video is still up on youTube but available only to people who have a direct link. Scheduled videos are stored for later publishing.

5. To upload the video you can click the large arrow to select the file, or you can simply click and drag the file directly from your computer.

6. While waiting for the video to upload fill in the information such as the title, description, and tags.

7. To complete the process click "Publish". For this, you don't even have to wait for the video to finish uploading. However, your video will not appear online unless you click Publish.

8. Depending on how long your video is, YouTube will need some time to process it. It can take up to a few minutes for your video to become available to your audience.

Uploading a video using the mobile app:

1. Launch the YouTube app on your device

2. At the top of the screen, you will find the upload button, tap it. Your device will ask you for permission to access your camera and photo library, allow it.

3. The next screen will take you to where your videos are stored. Choose the one you want to upload. At this point, you can also access your camera and start recording a new video, or opt to go live.

4. Select "Next".

5. Enter the information of your videos such as the title, description, and tags. At this point, you need to choose a privacy setting of your video- Public, Private, Unlisted, or Scheduled. Then tap "Upload" at the top of the screen and you are done.

Your videos are uploaded and ready to be seen by millions of people all around the globe!

Section 4: Growing Your YouTube Channel

Chapter 9: Your YouTube Audience

People chose to become successful YouTubers because they want to put themselves out there, and they want to be seen and to interact with the viewers. But who are exactly these viewers and how do you get them to see your videos? YouTube attracts 1.9 billion users each month. That is almost ⅔ of overall internet users. They all watch videos and enjoy the content YouTube has to offer, but they are not all the same. Every person will search for what interests them. It can be news, entertainment, tutorials and how-to's, or product reviews. Among younger generations, YouTube became a substitute for television. They don't get their information or entertainment from TV. They turn to online media and YouTube. But if they all have different interests, and search for different videos on YouTube, how do you get them to see yours? After all, viewers have billions of videos to watch, and how can you get all those people to choose your video among myriads of others? It is not a simple task, and you should avoid creating content for everyone. You should strive to create a loyal fanbase, made out of people who share an interest (or more) and attract them to subscribe to your channel.

The YouTube Community

Simply put, your audience, the viewers of your videos, are the people interested in watching the content of your channel. Not every viewer will become your audience. Your videos can be seen by people who will never again return to your channel as they are simply not interested in the type of videos you are making. Remember that they are not your audience, they are only passing by. You should never strive to please them. Concentrate on people who genuinely want to see the type of videos you are making. They are the reason behind your success, they are loyal to you, and they are here to stay. Your audience is your community, and once you determine what type of videos you want to make, it is time to determine what type of people you should strive to attract and subscribe to your channel.

Youtube is used by both men and women, by the elderly, and by children. The demographics of the viewers are vast. But still, the analytical data shows that YouTube is no place for bursting the stereotype bubbles. The majority of the audience is male, between 18 and 25 years old, and they mostly search for entertainment. This doesn't mean you should create content just for this type of audience. YouTube users are actually divided fairly equally between males and females. The only difference here is that males tend to spend more time on YouTube. The same goes for the age difference. Younger people tend to stay on youTube longer than the older ones. And it is true that women mostly search for beauty and fashion channels, while men prefer sport, gaming, and news channels. However, if you take gaming as a large category the divide between male and female viewers is 50-50. The same goes for lifestyle channels, if observed as a large category it attracts an equal part of male and female viewership. This demographic divide is most obvious when it comes to small niches. The narrower your niche is, it will attract specific kinds of demographics. You will notice that older men prefer sport, while younger ones prefer console gaming. Older women prefer storytelling channels while younger girls like make-up tutorials. There is only one niche that unites all of the youtube viewers. No matter the age, gender, or where on the planet earth they are located, everyone loves pets!

Knowing your audience will greatly help you determine who is watching your videos, and what type of videos you should strive to make. But never address your audience presuming you know them. Never address their age, their gender, or their location. Don't presume only men watch your videos because you are making only "let's play" type of content. Not only will you offend some of your viewers, but you will also lose the majority of them. People don't like to be generalized and put into categories.

Where Do Viewers Come From

Attracting the audience to your YouTube channel is not as simple as creating quality videos that will interest them. People still need to find your videos, and you need to learn how to reach them. To do this, you need to find out how the people learn about your video and where they are coming from. Did they search for your channel's name on YouTube or Google search bar, or did they follow an external link to your channel? If you know where the majority of your traffic is coming from, you will be able to create a promotion strategy and attract even more subscribers.

There are ways to see how people found your channel. For example, YouTube Analytics has an option to show you the traffic source types report. Through it, you can discover from which external websites and apps viewers came to your videos. Or see what videos they were watching when you came up as suggested. Youtube also allows its users to create playlists, and perhaps through some of them, your audience found you. Analytics will allow you to see the playlists that led viewers to your videos. In the end, you can always see what phrases did the viewers search for in YouTube's search bar when they found your video.

Understand that more than half of your viewers will come from search and suggestions simply because that is how YouTube's algorithm works. There is nothing much you can do about it, the algorithm is out of your hands. However, this only underlines the importance of optimization and metadata on your channel. Search and suggestions love good titles that are clearly describing what your video is about. The more accurately you do your SEO it is more likely for your video to show up in brows results and suggestions.

External and Embedded player traffic will tell you more about where your videos are being shared, which external websites are leading to your videos. YouTube Analytics will include other social media in its report and you will easily find out if your audience prefers Facebook, Twitter, or some other platform. Once you find that out, you can start sharing your videos on those platforms and generate even more traffic.

Getting People to Subscribe and Hit that Notification Icon

On YouTube, success is measured in numbers: of views, likes, and subscribers. You might ask yourself why are subscribers important? Isn't it enough to have as many views as possible? The answer is that subscribers are your viewers, but they are also the force behind your video that will get you even more views. Once again, it all boils down to the YouTube algorithm. The subscribers bump up the number of how many times your video was played, they also increase the watch time and the engagement. The YouTube algorithm will notice this and rank your videos higher making it able to reach new viewers easier. The more time your subscribers spend on your video, YouTube will consider its content relevant and will put it as a suggestion to the new viewers.

Having a large number of subscribers is also important if you want to monetize your videos. After all, you can't even start benefiting from the ad revenues if you have less than 1,000 subscribers. The more subscribers you have, the more money you can make from YouTube as the platform will offer you benefit levels. But if you don't want to become famous, viral, and successful, if you want to use YouTube as a digital marketing strategy for your already existing brand, you still need subscribers and you still want to up their numbers. The reason is simple, more subscribers mean more views. More views lead to new audiences and your videos will reach more people who will learn about your brand, and what you have to offer. Sure, you can always opt to buy YouTube subscribers, but that is not a good option. Bought subscribers are bots, and they are there only to pump the subscriber numbers. But they don't engage, they won't pump your play numbers or watch time. YouTube even has a fake engagement policy that will penalize you for using the bot subscribers. And finally, your real audience wants engagement, not only with you but also with other subscribers. And if all you have to offer them are bots, the real subscribers will leave because of the lack of engagement.

Buying YouTube subscribers is simply not worth it. But how do you get real ones? Here is a short series of advice on how to attract people to subscribe and how to get them for free.

1. Ask! Sometimes the best strategy is the simplest one. Ask your viewers to subscribe to your channel. Do it after you make your audience laugh, or learn something new, or do it at the end of the video. You don't need to ask them to subscribe every minute of your video, you will risk putting your audience off. Once is enough. You can personally ask by recording yourself, or you can write a text. The viewers sometimes need a reminder, and if they liked your content, they will want to return to it. Also, remind them to turn on notifications to receive reminders about your new videos.

2. Create anticipation. End your videos with a teaser of what you are working on

next. This will intrigue your viewers and they will want to come back and see what's next. They will subscribe in order to have a reminder to watch your next video.

3. Form a relationship with your audience. Engage your viewers and be friendly towards them. Respond to comments and follow them back. People genuinely appreciate the engagement and will want to come back to your channel.

4. You can run a contest. Offer your viewers a prize that will intrigue them, and mention that they need to be subscribed and that they need to turn on notifications in order to participate in the contest. Be fair, and reward your viewers for their loyalty.

5. Partner up with other channels. We already talked about collaboration with other YouTubers. It really works and it will bump your views and you will gain new subscribers.

6. Don't miss an opportunity to partner up with celebrities. Whether they are Youtube or other celebrities, it doesn't matter. This is a hard one, you need to

attract the celebrity to your channel, make them want to work with you. But if you make it work, the number of your subscribers will skyrocket.

Engaging with Your Audience

To build your YouTube community, increase the number of your subscribers, and attract new viewers, you need to devote some time to audience engagement. By doing so, you will turn them into loyal fans and they will anticipate your videos not only for their high quality but also because they feel valued and cherished by you. Keep in mind that there is a wrong way of engaging your audience, and it will leave them frustrated, disappointed and they will unsubscribe. But you might still wonder what the audience engagement actually is. It is the actions that your audience takes on your YouTube page, or on the page of one of your videos. These actions can be comments, likes, and dislikes, shares, new subscriptions, or unsubscriptions.

Don't expect the audience to engage just because you have an awesome video. There are many awesome videos out there, and you need to show that yours is worth their time. You will do this by reaching out first. Initiate the interaction with the audience by answering their comments under your video, or on other social media. Listen to their advice and concerns, put an effort into your reply. This will show that you value their opinion and will make them want to come back to you. You can also use your video to call the audience to action. Simply say that you would love to hear their opinion and that you can't wait to read their comments. This is a call to a conversation and the audience will be eager to start one. Another way to initiate action is to ask your audience for the ideas for your next video. Ask them what they would like to see, or if they have some questions for you.

Rewarding your loyal fans is always a good way to make the audience engage. You can organize competitions or giveaways. You can include in-video shoutouts, where you would personally thank your audience by mentioning some of their names. Feel free to go even further and ask them to participate in your next video. You can even organize meetups, and personally get to know some of your fans. Organize it online, through skype, hangouts or any other platform. Finally, join a cause and promote it through your videos. You will find that many of your viewers will appreciate the gesture. Raise money for a charity, invite guests to your channel to talk about climate change, or bring in the animal shelter workers to promote adoption. By promoting the cause you are passionate about, you will connect with your audience and they will want to engage on your page.

Tinkering with the Community Settings

Once you reach 1,000 subscribers, you will open access to Community Tab (it will replace the Discussion tab), which allows you to interact with your viewers using rich media. This means you will be able to create polls, to send text, images, and videos to your community. The community posts will allow you to interact with your subscribers separately from the videos on your channels. The Community Tab will appear in Home or in the Subscription feed allowing you easy access. The community tab is a Facebook-like experience where you can post status updates, or simply chat with your viewers or share gifs and images with them. But you should know that the visitors to your page can answer your posts only by text. Your subscribers will be notified of new community posts if they turn on notifications for your channel. In fact, try introducing your Community Tab in your next video, link it and invite your viewers to subscribe and turn on notifications. Here is how you can use Community Tab in different ways and for different purposes:

1. Your first community post should state its purpose. Welcome your audience and let them know what your intentions are. This will help you build a strong and loyal community.

2. You can always use community posts to market your product. You can post an image of your product, and include a link to your online store. Offer special discounts for your subscribers and advertise upcoming sales.

3. Promote your latest or next video. Post a teaser image or a short trailer that will announce your next video. If you have already published one, you can use community posts to link it.

4. Promote your old videos to the new audience. Even the old subscribers might enjoy remembering your previous content.

5. Use polls to find out what your audience thinks. This is an interesting feature that will allow you an insight into the mind of your audience, and maybe even help you prepare for your next video.

6. Host a Q&A on your Community Tab, or use it to promote your upcoming live Q&A video session.

7. Ask your audience some questions and let them be the creative drive behind your videos. Ask them for ideas and suggestions.

8. Share gifs and memes. This will allow you to connect with your audience on a more personal level. Nothing connects people quicker than a good laugh.

9. Promote a cause through your Community Tab, and rally your followers to the cause. You can even gather donations for a charity through community posts.

10. Use the community tab to post other people's channels. It is an excellent way of promoting your collaborations and channel partners. Drive the traffic their

way through your Community Tab and they will do the same for you.

Consider Doing a Livestream

YouTube has an option for live streaming and it is a great way to reach your audience in real-time. Going live means your video will be housed in the Live section and it will attract the viewers who are interested in seeing their favorite YouTubers in real-time. Of course, not only those who are interested in live content will see it. Anyone who subscribed to your channel, or anyone who watched one of your videos, or videos of other people but similar to yours, will have your live content suggested to them by YouTube. Going live is a special way of engaging the audience because there will be many viewers, all watching it at the same time. It will give them the experience and excitement of live events, but this time, made especially for their eyes. Live is a very unique way of presenting your content. Even if you are selling a product or promoting a brand, going live will get you a new audience, or make you stand out because you are doing it in such a unique way.

YouTube Live is a very popular option and the numbers are there to support this claim. More than 80% of adults prefer live videos instead of reading a blog post or the news. Around 82% of adults prefer to watch live videos than to browse through social media posts. 70% of the adults claim YouTube is their favorite platform for live content. These numbers make it obvious why you should consider going live. This doesn't mean you should do it all the time, but keep it occasionally, when you feel inspired or have a need for it.

Keep in mind that you can't just simply go live and expect people to watch you. You will need to do some promotion of your live event, just like a concert needs one. There are several ways of promoting your live event. The most obvious one is getting the word out there through social media. Everyone is on Facebook, Twitter, or Instagram. You can even use your Community Tab on YouTube to announce and promote your live streaming. You can even opt for Facebook advertising campaigns to give your promotional campaign a little extra push. The good thing is that you can limit your expenditure on ads and keep them as small as you want, but still secure viewership through them. Just make sure you post advertisements and promotions on time. Do it at least several days in advance.

Now that you planned and promoted your live streaming session, it is time to consider what you can do to ensure its success. First of all, brainstorm the content of your live video. Just as if you would do it with a recorded one. You can't go in front of the camera unprepared and rely only on your good looks and skills. If you are doing a live Q&A, be certain to prepare some rules and explain to your audience how it is going to work. Encourage your viewers to participate in the live stream. To do this, enable the real-time chat function and ask your audience for an opinion, or their suggestion. Encourage them to ask you questions. Make your live stream fun! Maybe your priority is to inform your audience, but that doesn't mean you should be completely professional. The audience will expect live streams to be fun and enjoyable and you should give your best to give them that experience. Be creative, play a little game with your audience, or tell a funny story from your life.

Chapter 10: Managing Your Channel

In this section, you will learn how to get the most out of your channel. Making and publishing high-quality videos is just one-half of the job and being a Youtuber also means running many channel-related tasks that are not at all creative, but necessary to keep you going and reach success. In his chapter, you will learn how the YouTube Algorithm works, how to make the best out of it, and what other options are out there when it comes to owning your own YouTube channel.

Welcoming Your Audience to the Channel

Once a potential viewer comes to your channel for the first time, he will want to see all that you have to offer in one place. The best place to do that little presentation is a channel trailer video. It is exactly like a movie trailer, it will quickly present all that your channel stands for, and tease the viewer making him want to see more. The trailer for your YouTube channel will directly influence the viewers' decision whether to subscribe or not. This is why the trailer needs to make an impact on the audience, and hook them up! If you wonder what should go into your trailer video here is a quick guideline:

1. Welcome the audience to your channel. Treat your channel as your home, you want the guests to feel comfortable. The best way to do it is to address them personally and welcome them.

2. Assume they are visiting your channels page for the first time. Many of them will be there for the first time, and your trailer video should be targeting them. Introduce yourself, or your brand and make them see what you have to offer.

3. Tell your viewers why they should subscribe and ask them to do so. When the video finishes, your video will have an end card that will enable the viewers to subscribe immediately.

4. Plan your trailer video and write a script. Decide what the tone of your trailer video should be and what emotions do you want the audience to feel upon watching it.

5. Add graphics and music to make your video more attractive and engaging. This will help draw in your audience and make them want to see what content you can offer them.

6. Although there is no perfect length for the trailer video, you will want to keep it short. Think of movie trailers, they are ace paced and short. The length should be just enough to intrigue the viewer, spark and interest, but not reveal too much because the real content is waiting for them in your other videos.

7. Use storytelling powers. This doesn't mean that you should bore them to death with talk. Instead, use imagery to tell the story. After all, most viewers prefer visual stimulus. Keep away from using written text in your trailer video.

8. The first few seconds of the trailer video are crucial. That is when the viewer's attention gets hooked or not. The intro of your trailer should be interesting and engaging. Start with a fun fact, or a question that will make your audience wonder.

Make Use of Playlists

If you can think of it, YouTube has a playlist for it. Your favorite music band, or the funniest scenes from the Simpsons, there is a playlist for that. YouTube playlists are an awesome way of engaging your audience and you should use them to grow your brand and to maximize your marketing strategy. But first, you need to learn what is a YouTube playlist, and how to use it. A YouTube playlist is a set of videos that play in order. When one video finishes, the next one will start automatically. Users don't have to take any action to play the next video. All they have to decide is which playlist will suit their momentary needs. Do they need to cheer up? Maybe they will search for a funny video playlist. Do they need relaxing music for work? There is a playlist with all the mellow, chill, and relaxing tunes that will help a person concentrate.

But for YouTube content creators, the playlists are the ultimate content curation tool. This means that you can use a playlist to engage your audience, instead of doing it with just one video. The playlist does need to tell a story and you should avoid putting together a playlist of random videos. The viewer's experience will be enhanced because he doesn't have to do any content search. The possibilities for playlists are endless, and the way you will use them is all up to you. You can put together all the Q&As you did in the past. Or pair videos that address the same topic. Make two separate playlists of funny dog's videos and funny cat's videos for the audience that is interested only in their favorite animal.

To create a playlist on YouTube, simply go to "My Channel". Select the "Customize Channel" option to access the video manager. This screen allows you to edit your entire YouTube channel including the description, banners, and videos. Now select the "Playlist" tab in the middle of the screen and click on the button "New playlist" to create a new one. Enter the title for the playlist you are making and click "Create" (the title can always be edited later, in case you change your mind). Now that you created a playlist, it's time to add videos to it. Click the "edit" button then "Add videos" and simply select the ones you want to use. Now that your playlist contains some videos in it, it's time to share it with the rest of the world. Do this by simply clicking the "Share" button. You can share it through email, social media platforms, or embed it in your website or blog post. Creating a playlist is simple and YouTube's interface will allow you to do it in no time. Why not use this awesome feature and make it easier for your viewers to find the videos of their interest?

Are You Properly Utilizing YouTube Stories?

If you manage to get 10,000 subscribers, YouTube will enable you to share stories with your fans. They are short, mobile-only videos that will offer you the opportunity to connect with your audience in a unique, casual, and "in the spur of the moment" way. Use the stories to engage your audience and make them into your loyal subscribers. Stories will be visible for only 7 days, and then YouTube will remove them. The concept is similar to Facebook and Instagram stories, but it will offer you a dynamic way to connect directly to your YouTube audience, without using other social media platforms. Keep in mind that if your channel is labeled to be for children, this feature will not be available to you. You will be able to add stickers to your stories and to interact with your audience through comments and replies, and you will have direct influence over the short video and delete it even before the 7 days time period expires.

YouTube stories can be created only through the YouTube Play app, and not through YouTube Creator Studio. This is what makes them a perfect marketing solution for smartphone users. You can add images or videos to your story from your phone's library, or you can create them on the go. Remember that story videos can be only 15 seconds long, so whatever content you choose to put, make it short and to the point. You can add music, use filters, insert links and add text and stickers to your story. Once you are happy with the end result, tap Save and only then tap Post and your story will be delivered to your audience.

As a content creator on YouTube, you have to strategize the use of the stories. Use them to engage the audience, ask them questions, and get inspired by their answers. Build a relationship with your audience by addressing their comments personally. Hit a reply button and answer their questions, or compliment their insight. Use the YouTube story to announce your newest video, or to advertise your products. Stories are a great way to market your brand, especially because you can add links to them. They will ensure your main websites get organic traffic too.

How YouTube Videos are Ranked

More than 300 hours of video per minute are being uploaded on YouTube at any given time. It is hard to get noticed and to succeed as a content creator. While offering quality content will guarantee that your audience will return, it is the SEO that will attract the audience to your video in the first place. In order to do a proper SEO, you need to understand how YouTube ranks the videos. In this section, you will learn the most important ranking factors that you will continuously use to optimize your presence on YouTube. Optimized YouTube channel will help search engines understand the content of your video, and increase its ranking both on YouTube search pages and within search engines such as Google.

Keywords

YouTube's algorithm pays much attention to the metadata of your video. The keywords you choose to use are a significant part of the metadata. Keywords are simple, one or two-word descriptions of your channel or your video, and just by glancing at them, the users will know what your content is about. Keywords can be added through the advanced setting in the Creator Studio within YouTube itself. You have to understand the importance of the proper use of keywords. They are effective only if they are carefully chosen and relate closely to your brand, the niche, and the content of your videos. This is why you should always do some keyword research before choosing them. There are many useful tools that can help you with keyword research, such as Google AdWords Keyword Planner or Rank Tracker.

Pay special attention to how many keywords you are using. If used in great numbers, they will start diluting the importance of each one of them. Keep it in between 5 to 10. To get some ideas for your channel keywords visit your competitor's channels and see what works for them. Another method of finding the right keywords to use is YouTube search suggestion. Start typing a phrase relevant to your channel and see what YouTube will suggest to you. These keywords are great for the simple reason that you don't have to wonder if they are popular. If YouTube is suggesting them, it means people actually search for them. If you are recording the speech for your content, say your keywords during the video. Make them fit in the content naturally. This is important because YouTube automatically transcribes your videos and uses this transcription to understand its content.

Video Title and Description

As you already know, metadata is extremely important for YouTube to rank your videos properly, and the titles are part of the metadata. This is why you should pay close attention to how you title your content. Titles give a first impression about your video, not only to the viewers but also to search engines and YouTube itself. A video with a good title will attract more traffic to your channel and will increase the number of views your videos will have. Shorter titles work better because the long ones often get cut off in the search bar. Try to limit your titles to five words or less. Your main keyword should be at the start of the title, and it should be the most relevant one for the content of your video.

The video description is very similar to the title of the video, but the good thing is you have more room for keywords. The description will help Google and YouTube understand the content of your video. Start the description with the most relevant keywords and keep it at least 250 words long. Include links to your other social media, blog, or website in the description and you will helpYouTube rank you higher. Don't be afraid to repeat the keywords in the description, but this doesn't mean you should make a list. The descriptionn should be relevant to the readers too. Try to limit your repetitive keywords to 2 to 4 times. Avoid being spammy, and be as informative as you can.

Video Tags

Tags are short, one or two words, descriptions that will help YouTube understand the topic and the content of your video. Tags generally don't have the impact on the ranking as keywords do, but they still play an important role. They will not only help the search engine rank your video, but they will also help users find it. Tags are keywords and it is important to use the words and phrases you think users might search for. Keep them relevant to your video, otherwise, they won't do their job. If you are doing beauty tutorials, make sure to use tags such as "make-up tutorial", "evening make-up", or "home beauty treatment". Keep the number of the tags in mind. You don't have to type a whole bunch of them. Ten well thought tags will do a better job than 20 irrelevant ones.

Tags may not be the most important thing when it comes to YouTube rankings, but they do play a role in making your video a suggested one or a related video in the sidebar area. If a viewer is watching a video about gaming from another channel, if your tags are relevant, YouTube will suggest to that viewer to watch your gaming video next.

Video Quality

YouTube loves HD videos and promotes them. Any video, on any given topic, will rank higher if it's in HD. But the quality of your video will have the most important impact on the user's experience. High-Quality videos attract more traffic, and the more traffic you have, the higher your video will rank. YouTube focuses on users' interaction with the videos because it can't use backlinks like Google does to determine the relevance of your content. If the user's engagement is negative, your video will rank lower. But High-Quality videos don't necessarily mean HD. You can have the viewers spend more time watching, commenting, and liking your videos if you offer them quality content. This means that no matter how well you do your SEO, if your video has no quality to offer (resolution, content, or both), it will not rank well.

User Experience Metrics

In the Video Quality section, we mentioned the importance of users interacting with your channel and your videos. YouTube simply places a lot of focus on this interaction when determining how to rank a video. It uses several metrics to do so: comments, number of new subscribers after watching the video, likes and dislikes, and shares. YouTube uses these numbers as a basis on which to determine the quality of your video and its relevance. Videos that are capable of engaging the users, making them like, share and comment, will definitely rank higher. The time a viewer spends watching your video is also important and falls into this category. If your video is 10 minutes long, but the user stops watching it after only one minute, YouTube will receive a signal that your video content is not interesting, of no relevance, and will rank it lower.

Closed Captions

If you use spoken words in your videos, you should consider using closed captions. There are two major reasons why you should do this:

1. Your videos will become available to a much larger community, as the people who do not speak your language or are deaf, will now be able to follow it.

2. Search Engines analyze closed captions and include their value in the ranking system.

YouTube will offer you the option to upload your own subtitles, or to use automatic captioning. The automatic one is not perfect and in order to ensure the overall quality of your video, it is recommended to upload your own.

Mastering YouTube Analytics

A tool that content creators use to measure the success of their YouTube marketing efforts is called YouTube Analytics. You can access this tool from the YouTube Studio dashboard, it is integrated with the YouTube website, and you don't need to do any installation on your part. This tool is capable of tracking everything that is going on on YouTube, but that doesn't mean you need to have an insight into everything that exists. YouTube Analytics works with raw data, and if you don't know how to translate it, what's the point? You should concentrate on observing the data that helps you turn a viewer into a subscriber. Understand what your audience values, and how to keep them engaged, and you will hit a jackpot.

To use YouTube Analytics, you need to log in to your YouTube account, click your profile icon, select YouTube Studio and then select Analytics. In the upper right corner select Advanced Mode for a detailed breakdown of the channel and video data. Now you can opt to download this information, directly from the Advanced Mode. You can also click the Compare To option in the upper right corner and this will take you to a new screen where you will be given insight into various parameters, past and present, and you will be able to compare them.

Youtube metrics

To be able to read all the data YouTube Analytics presents to you, you will need to learn each metric measured, why is it important, and how to use this data to improve your performance.

Subscribers: This represents the number of people that subscribed to your channel. YouTube Analytics will allow you to see how many new subscribers you gained over a certain period. To see how this figure compares to your typical subscriber growths, simply however over its icon.

Realtime views: This is the number of views your last published video received in the period of the last 48 hours. This metric is an excellent way of tracking how well your YouTube Live or recently published video performed.

Top Videos: will display a snapshot of the videos that performed the best over a given period of time. YouTube Analytics will allow you to adjust the time frame, and you can easily conclude which of your videos is the all-time best performer.

Channel Views: This will allow you to track how many times your channel was viewed over a given period of time. You can compare different periods and determine if your channel performed better in the past or in the present. If you notice your view counts are lower now, you may see what you did well in the past and repeat it to attract the audience back to your channel.

Channel Watch Time: will give you tidal hours people have spent on your channel. You can compare this number to the average watch time simply by hovering over the icon.

Audience Metrics

To better understand your viewers, use audience metrics. It will help you adjust your content and community management and digital marketing strategies/

Unique viewers: This represents the number of people who watched your video at a selected period of time. This metric doesn't include multiple views that come from the same person.

Average views per viewer: This is a metric that tells you the number of times one viewer watched a video on your channel. It will include multiple views of one video, and the views of multiple videos.

When your viewers are on YouTube: This is a chart that displays days and hours that have the most viewers on your channel. This info is important because you can base your publishing schedule according to it.

Audience demographics: This will let you know the age, gender, and location of your audience. Use this information to plan the content or your viewers, or maybe even content that will attract the demographics missing from your channel.

Youtube Discovery Metrics

This metric will allow you to learn how people find your videos and how they discover your channel. Whether they visited your channel through external links or found it by using the YouTube search bar. Learning these metrics will help you to adjust your SEO.

Impressions and CTR: Each time someone sees the thumbnail of your video, the impression is recorded. But impression click-through rates will display the number of people who clicked on the thumbnail to access the video. If you have a high click-through rate, that means your keywords and your thumbnails are effective. But in order to see how the video itself is performing, you will need to see the watch time and average view duration.

Traffic sources: will tell you where and how people find your videos. Traffic sources include YouTube search, suggestions, and playlists. Other sources are measured too, and you can find out if people used Direct URLs or External links.

Top YouTube search terms: you can see these if you go to Traffic Source and then YouTube Search. This is how you will find out the top searched terms that people used to find your videos. This will give you a clue if your SEO strategy is performing well, or if it needs adjusting.

YouTube Video Metrics

This section will help you track the metrics for a certain video and determine how well it performs. Based on the data collected, you can conclude what you need to do differently in your future videos to perform better.

Views: This metric shows you the number of times a video has been watched overall. This includes repeated views from the same person.

Video Subscribers: This represents the number of people who subscribed to your channel after watching a particular video.

Watch Time: This will tell you how much time people spend watching your video overall. This number is accumulated after a certain period of time.

Audience retention: This metric will tell you how far people made it through your video. It is an average view duration, and you will learn at what point of the video people lose interest.

YouTube Engagement Metrics

This section will tell you how and when your audience is engaging with your channel. Use it to plan interaction with the audience, such as replies to comments, or asking them to subscribe, like, and share.

Likes and dislikes: Sometimes they are considered vanity metrics, but they are important. They will tell you what people think of your content and if you need to change something to perform better.

Card and end screen reports: These reports will display the metrics for the interactive content you added to your video. The report from this secretion will tell you if they worked, and which cards worked best.

YouTube Revenue Metrics

This section is very important to the content creators who monetize their videos, as it will help them track their earnings.

Estimated revenue: This will tell you how much your channel earned during a specific period of time. The figure you get includes all sources of revenue.

Revenue sources: This metric will display a breakdown of all the sources your videos use to make money through YouTube.

Let's Talk About Copyright

YouTube takes copyright very seriously, and you should mind how you use the intellectual property of other people. But before you understand why this is important, you need to know what copyright is and how you can avoid copyright infringement. When a person creates an original work, be it music, sound, image, or written word, he automatically owns the copyright to this work. That means he is the only one who can make copies of his own work. But he can also give the right to others to use his work. The copyright law is different in different countries, but YouTube takes it very seriously.

The laws are set in place to protect the creators and their work, and give them certain rights. If a musician allows his work to be used without any copyright protection, he wouldn't be able to make a living out of his own music. Here are the types of works that are subjected to copyright:

1. Musical compositions and any sound recording

2. Audiovisual works such as TV shows, online videos, music videos, movies, etc

3. Visual work such as photographs, posters, paintings, etc

4. Video games and computer software

5. Written works such as articles, books, poems, musical compositions, etc

6. Dramatic works such as musicals, scripts, and plays

It is important to understand that facts, processes, and ideas are not subjected to copyright. It may be immoral to steal an idea, but the deed itself is not protected by copyright laws. Only creative works fixed in a physical medium are eligible for copyright. But be cautious, as anything else can be protected by patent and trademark laws.

YouTube punishes the users who infringe on copyright. The video that is violating other people's copyright will be taken down, and the user will be punished by a strike. If a user gets three strikes YouTube will take away your channel. There are precautionary measures you can take in order to ensure this doesn't happen to you.

Have permission. The rules are simple, everything you created belongs to you and you own the copyright. But if you choose to upload the content created by another person, you better have their permission to use it. Remember that copyright is not only created as soon as the work is done. It is also in place for as long as the creator lives, and even some time after his death. That means that there are some intellectual works out there that are open for public use and you are free to use them.

If you decide to use someone else's work you need to get their permission. Simply stating that something was created by someone else, or adding the name of the copyright owner is not enough. This is still a breach that will lead to video being blocked, and you get a strike from YouTube. What you need to do to be able to use someone else's work is to get a license for it. However, the licenses often come with some kind of restrictions. It might be that the license states that no monetization is to be made through the use of the copyrighted material, or that you can use it only for a limited time. Be sure to read the rights and limitations of such licenses in detail.

There is always an option of Fair Use. This is when you copy the copyrighted material for a limited, and transformative purpose. In other words, you are allowed to comment, criticize or make a parody out of copyrighted material. This can be done without the permission of the author of the copyrighted material. However, Fair Use is somewhat tricky, because it can be implemented only in videos that are out there to inform or educate. You cannot monetize from Fair Use.

Chapter 11: YouTube and SEO in a Nutshell

Not so long ago, the internet became a perfect place for all types of marketing. At first, it was enough to publish a high volume of marketing material in order to secure the views and traffic. However, with the increase of internet use, it became impossible to find relevant information in a sea of content out there. Search engines had to be modified and made able to filter relevant material from the spam content. Various algorithms were made to do this filtering and the marketers had to change their tactics. Suddenly, the volume wasn't enough and they had to produce high-quality content which would also be optimized in such a way that search engines would discover it and rank it high on the result pages. Only several years ago the algorithms were able to work only with the written word. But now they are able to work with videos, images, and even sounds. Through smart optimization of text, sound, images, and video, you can make your content rank high. This is what SEO is all about and why you should do it properly.

SEO, in General

SEO stands for Search Engine Optimization and in simple terms, it means improving your internet presence (through website, blog, YouTube channel, etc), to increase its visibility. The truth is, you need to rank high in order to be noticed by the users who search for the content you are creating. When using search engines such as Google, people pay close attention only to the first page. This is not because they are lazy, but because search engines rank the relevance of the content. This means that the first result displayed is probably there because of high-quality content that will satisfy the consumers. The further down you go, the displayed results lose in relevance. Your goal as a content creator must be to show up on the first page of the search engine, and if possible, to show up as the first result.

But how do search engines know what is high-quality content? Simply put, they were designed to crawl pages on the web and collect information. They index the information and analyze it. There are hundreds of ranking factors the algorithm would use in order to determine the order in which the pages should be displayed. Some of them are the usage of keywords, the construction of the content (if it was written for humans or for machines), and even the architecture of the website (if it was constructed for browser use or if they are also mobile-friendly). you can take into account all of these factors and create a website, or a YouTube channel that would help you rank higher on the search results page. The search engine algorithms are constantly evolving, learning, and changing in order to give the users the best experience. This is why SEO is a marketing branch that requires constant updates and adjustments to the work routine.

How SEO Works on YouTube

SEO for YouTube is a little bit different than for search engines like Google or Bing. This is because instead of using backlinks, YouTube prefers to analyze the user experience and determine the quality of the content based on that. That means that if your YouTube video engages the audience, if its content makes them stay, subscribe or interact with your channel and video in any other way, it will rank it better. In chapter 10 we discussed the importance of user experience metrics and how to comment count, the length of the video, the number of views, likes, shares, etc will influence how you rank on YouTube. You should dedicate your time to improve your user engagement methods and attract your audience to subscribe and stay on your channel. But there are other things you could also be doing in order to improve your rankings and here is what theta re:

1. Keyword research. By now you understand the importance of having a good set of keywords that will be related to your content and describe it in the best possible way so that search engines will understand what your videos are about. However, you should pay special attention to researching your keywords often and with the right tools. The popularity of keywords changes over time and a keyword that worked perfectly yesterday might not work for you tomorrow. This is why it is important to periodically check your keywords and how they rank. Google provides you with a free tool you can use to check the popularity of the keywords and discover new ones. It's called "Google Trends" and it already comes with a YouTube search option implemented.

2. Track the rankings of your videos on YouTube. You don't need to do this manually, there are tools out there, both

free and paid, that will help you keep track of your positioning on both Google and on YouTube. One such tool is Ubersuggest.

3. Be consistent. While becoming viral is a great thing, it will bring you a short burst of fame. The key is consistency. You need to build your subscribers base and turn your viewers into fans. This can be done only over a long period of time. Keep producing high-quality videos that are published on schedule. Having two viral videos in a row is impossible, and forget about making all of your videos viral. Only by building a strong community of viewers and through their engagement with your channel, you will have a consistently high ranking.

4. While it is true most people will give a video maybe a minute or two to intrigue them, that doesn't mean you should keep your videos short. Put the most intriguing information at the beginning, but keep the video at least five minutes long. Google ranks better longer videos because it means they can charge for more advertisement. High-quality, long-

form content allows running more ads, therefore more profit for YouTube.

5. The first 48 hours are critical. Prepare your SEO before you publish a video. Better yet, before you upload it. Never publish a video without properly done SEO, thinking you can do it anytime you want. As soon as you give YouTube's algorithm the information about what your video is about, it will rank high enough to attract viewers. These viewers will interact with your video through likes, comments, and subscriptions, and will push its rankings even higher. The sooner this happened the better. It is possible to go back and repair the SEO of your older videos to keep them relevant. But once the algorithm judges your video, it is very hard to change that judgment.

Applying & Improving SEO on Your Channel

To get the YouTube SEO right, you will need to dedicate a lot of time to optimize your channel, playlist, metadata for each video, their description, titles, thumbnails, and even the video content itself. It is important to think about your videos as text and even transform them into text. This will help you rank higher not only on YouTube but also on Google and other search engines. The power of transcripts, closed captions, and subtitles are not to be ignored. This is how search engines learn about the content of your videos and it is the text they use to process the information and decide how to rank the video. Here are some tricks you can apply in order to take your YouTube SEO skills to the next level:

1. Add Closed Captions. YouTube will automatically transcribe your videos, but its auto-caption is only 70% accurate. The mistakes it makes can influence the ranking of your videos as the search engine will not understand fully what your content is about. This is why it is important to provide YouTube with 100% accurate captions. But there is one more draw-back from automated-captions. Google will penalize you for using the random words as captions, as it will treat them as spam. If they sound like gibberish, and most likely they will, Google will decide the captions are unworthy and will rank your video lower.

2. Add the transcript of your video to its description. Since the description field allows you to type 4,850 characters (including spaces), this should be enough to fit a transcript of a dialog-heavy video that lasts up to 10 minutes. If your video is longer than that, you can make a short version of a transcript, but include a link to the full version on a separate web page. This is done because the description section of your videos is where the search engine's algorithms will crawl first in order to index your video.

3. Translate the video transcripts and captions in different languages. This is more important if your content is not in English, or if you are targeting a population from a certain location in order to expand your audience. Search engine algorithms will include the translated transcriptions and captions and rank your videos higher in the countries where those languages are native.

4. Use the video SEO embed in order to inject the video's metadata into the head of your webpage. This will allow search engines to crawl and index the video

properly. Try out 3Play Plugin to make the videos SEO-friendly. Optimizing your videos not only for YouTube but for search engines too will bring you more views. And even though Google prioritizes the videos on its search page, it won't be able to do so if the SEO is not done properly.

5. Use playlists and subcategorize your videos. Make playlists by grouping 4 to 6 relevant videos. This will not only increase the users' engagement, but it will also make it easier for your audience to share multiple videos at a time. This way, more of your videos will reach a new audience.

Chapter 12: YouTube Marketing

Social media marketing became a huge opportunity back in the early days of Facebook, Twitter, and Instagram. But recently, marketers are turning to YouTube as they see the great potential video marketing on social media has. After all, YouTube is a social media platform too, as well as the second largest search engine. With over 6 billion people using YouTube each day, marketers would lose so much if they chose to ignore it. Maintaining the presence on different social media is how businesses and brands reach out to their audience and how they engage with them. YouTube is nothing different. People from around the world use YouTube and this platform became a unique way for marketers to reach new audiences. Video marketing is increasing because video accounts for over 70% of internet traffic in general. In this section, you will learn how to use YouTube and advertise your brand or service and how it will help you grow your business by reaching new audiences.

The Basics of Marketing

Marketing is a set of activities one makes in order to sell or promote a product or a service. It is what you say in order to convince the people your product or service is worth their time and money. Marketing is not only advertising, it also includes the sale and the delivery of the product and service to the people. After all, you want your customers and clients to keep coming back to you. Because marketing is a complex idea that drives a business, there are third-party affiliates that do marketing professionally and offer their services to companies and businesses. Big companies usually have their own marketing departments that take care of the advertising and searching for new potential markets on which to sell their company's product. Promotion is not a synonym for marketing. It is just one of its branches. Promotion is marketing done on specifically targeted audiences in order to expand the business.

Marketing is not only about drawing in customers and clients. It is also about maintaining the relationship with the already existing ones. Keeping in touch with past clients, as well as reaching out to potential ones is an important part of marketing. It may even involve writing "thank you" notes, emails, sending gifts to prospective clients, and socializing with them. But people often think that marketing is about pushing the product just to everyone. However, it is more nuanced than that. Marketing is about matching the product with the people who need access to it. This is one of the reasons for the existence of the Four Ps of marketing: product, price, place, and promotion. When put together, these elements make up the essential mix a company needs in order to successfully market its product or service.

Product: This is the item or service a company wants to offer to the customers. Before trying to market the product, marketers need to understand it, and to learn how it compares to the same or similar products that the competing company is offering.

Price: The price is the amount of monetary value the company wants for its product. There are many factors that enter the process of establishing the price for a product or service: unit cost price, marketing costs, packaging, and distribution expenses.

Place: This is the location where the product will be distributed. This includes making a decision if the sale will be in a physical store or through online platforms.

Promotion: In other words, this is a marketing communication campaign. It includes advertising, selling, various sales, direct marketing, public sales, guerilla marketing (unconventional interactions with customers in order to promote a product), and sponsorship.

Online sales are increasing each year. Only in 2017, they reached an unbelievable 65% of total sales. Considering the lightning-fast increase in popularity of online sales, online marketing is a critical part of the overall marketing strategy. Digital advertising and the use of social media platforms have become a norm. Youtube has joined the world of digital marketing as both a place to host the advertisement and a place to reach a new audience, as well as to keep in touch with the already existing customers.

Social Media Marketing (SMM)

Social Media Marketing became one of the largest aspects of marketing. Because the general population is using social media platforms on a daily basis, it became incredibly important for businesses to reach their audience through Facebook, Twitter, Instagram, Youtube, etc. Social media platforms give the opportunity to brands and businesses to directly speak to their audience. If you are not doing it, you are missing out! It is not news that social media usage surpassed that of the TV or radio. Marketing on social media will bring great success to your business, but that doesn't mean it is an easy job. There are nuances to be used in order to maximize your social media outreach. Another difficulty is staying in trend. Social media platforms are ever-changing, and as social media marketer, you need to constantly be up to date and follow the rules of the game.

Social media marketing is a branch of Internet marketing and it involves creating content for social media which will ensure that the marketing and branding goals online are achieved. Activities that make up social media marketing include posting text, images, and video updates, in order to get the audience to engage. Another aspect of social media marketing is paid to advertise.

How SMM Works

Strategy: Social media marketing campaigns need to be planned in detail. But before you even start, you need to think about what are the goals of your business and what exactly do you want to achieve with the campaign. Only after you are certain you have these figured out, you can start planning your marketing strategy. If you start the marketing complaint without any plan, you will soon become lost and overwhelmed. Instead of aimlessly wandering the social media field, try asking yourself some of these questions, in order to determine how to define your social media marketing goals:

1. What is driving you to start a social media marketing campaign?

2. What do you think you will achieve with it?

3. Who is your targeted audience?

4. How would your targeted audience use social media?

5. Which platforms, groups, pages would they visit the most?

6. What is the message you want to send to your audience, through social media?

The type of your business will greatly influence your social media strategy. This means that if you are in the travel business section, you can opt to use highly visual stimuli to reach your audience. This means that the best social media platforms for your business would be Pinterest, or Instagram, as well as YouTube. Twitter or Linkedin would be a better option for a marketing company or business to business outreach.

When determining the goals of your social marketing strategy you should think about whether you want to raise awareness about your brand or to drive traffic and sales. Social media is an amazing place to create a community that would be encouraged to engage with your brand. This is why you should think about starting customer support through social media. And that will lead you to the next step in the thought process. Which social platform is perfect for your business. There are a lot of social media platforms, and although you should establish a presence on more than just one, that doesn't mean you should do it on all of them. Think about your targeted audience and where do you think they hang out the most?

Pick a few platforms which you know with certainty have the highest possibility of reaching your targeted audience, as well as satisfying your business goals. Facebook and Instagram are great for driving traffic and sales, but Twitter might be a better option for raising awareness.

Planning and Publishing: Once you have your strategy up, it is time to plan the content for your social media marketing. You need to think upfront about what you want this content to look like, will you use videos, images, GIFs, etc. You should also write a script and text for everything you plan to publish. Also, make a schedule for publishing and determine when exactly to publish each post. The timing and frequency of your publishing are incredibly important. You want to maximize the reach and you should determine at what days and at what times most of your audience is active on social media.

Listening and Engagement: Once you published your first social media posts, you should monitor how users and customers are interacting with it. Read comments, count the likes and shares, see if anyone tagged someone else to attract the attention of their family and friends to your business. Remember that people might talk about your brand or business without tagging you. You won't know when this happens, so you will need to do some manual search. However, this shouldn't be a difficult job. There are many tools out there that can help you monitor the engagement of your audience.

Analytics: If you want to know how your social media marketing is performing, you will have to analyze some raw data. This will tell you if you got any new followers, and what their number is compared to the previous month; or how many positive mentions you got. You will also know if people are using your brand's hashtag and if they are sharing your posts. The social platforms will provide you with some of the information you need, but to get the best results, you should consider using some of the tools specially designed to keep track of the analytics.

Advertising: Social media platforms allow you to post ads too. These are paid ads that will ensure you reach the widest possible audience. These social media advertising tools are so powerful that you can specify your targeted audience based on their location, gender, age, interests, and even based on their interaction with your competitors.

Marketing on YouTube

YouTube is a platform that reaches around 95% of the world's population, and it can be accessed in 76 different languages. It is no wonder the businesses are hurrying up to establish their presence on YouTube, and marketers are rushing to offer YouTube their services. You might think that YouTube is too narrowly specialized and that your audience is not there. But think again! Over ⅓ of the overall time people spend on the internet, they spend watching videos. YouTube has more than two billion active users, and the chances that your audience is there are great. Everyone uses youtube, even the elderly. And it's not only about reaching the audience. Correct use of SEO and YouTube can help you and your brand rank higher on different search engines. Most importantly, YouTube allows you to share unique content with your audience and ensure their engagement.

If you ever watched a video on YouTube, and the chances are that you did, you probably encountered YouTube ads. It is important that Marketing on YouTube isn't equal to running those ads. We will talk more about them in the next chapter. Now it is important you understand that marketing on YouTube means creating your own channel with the name of your brand, producing high-quality videos which will engage the audience and at the same time advertise your product. For example, you can host a Q&A session with your audience, or make an unboxing video, create tutorials on how to properly use the product you're selling, or simply make an intro class that will explain the service your business has to offer. The possibilities are enormous. Look at how other businesses did it. Some of the most famous make-up producers already have their presence established on YouTube and they are creating content for their viewers by hosting famous make-up artists.

If you are still not convinced that YouTube is perfect for your business, let's see three main reasons why you should seriously give it a chance:

1. Make your brand an authority in the field. Video marketing will help your audience build their trust in you. You will become a figure of authority to whom the viewers can always come back for the necessary information. Your presence on

YouTube will say "Hey! I'm always here for you", and the customers will find it easy to connect to your brand. People appreciate the help and value they are getting through these business-driven videos on YouTube and find it easy to connect with the ideas and strategies behind those businesses.

2. Build Credibility! When it comes to customer acquisition, trust is everything. If your audience doesn't trust you, they won't buy your product or your services. Because of this, you have to take steps to build a relationship with your audience, grow your customer base and keep them informed. Offering information is the best way to gain someone's trust. Through videos on YouTube, you can put a face behind the information, someone your audience can connect to on a more personal level, and the credibility will rise.

3. YouTube is more engaging than other social media platforms. People enjoy watching videos and they do it more now than ever before. Videos are entertaining and the viewer doesn't need to put much effort into finding what they like. Since

through videos you would be able to connect with your audience, you would step beyond the boundaries of traditional marketing. You can keep the communication between and your viewers going and add a personal touch to your brand's name. Make sure to reply to your viewers' comments and take their concerns and suggestions into consideration. Show them you care and they will become loyal followers and customers.

Branding on YouTube

If you are opening a YouTube channel especially for your business, you should consider several key points that make a difference between brand channel and personal channel. Your brand's channel is the extension of your business, and it should be treated professionally. Channel identity plays a major role in social media marketing. If you follow these few steps you will easily attract new subscribers and create a fanbase for your brand:

1. Channel name: The name of your brand's YouTube channel must reflect your

business's name, and be consistent on all social media platforms.

2. Channel icon: The YouTube channel icon is similar to the Facebook profile picture, but since YouTube is part of Google, it will be used across all of your Google properties. The best option for brands is to use a company logo or a professional headshot in case you are the face of your own brand.

3. Channel art: Make sure that you chose the size and image for your channel art that scales well on all devices. You never know what device your audience is using to access your channel, mobile phone, tablet, PC, or TV.

4. Channel description. This is the perfect place for you to provide the audience with a detailed description of your brand or your company. Explain what it is that you do, and what types of videos you plan to share with your viewers. Use relevant keywords at the beginning of your channel's description to ensure search engines rank you higher.

5. Channel trailer: Keep it short and sweet (between 30 and 60 seconds). Keep it

focused around your channel's idea, your business, and explain what your audience can expect to see. Don't forget to invite the viewers to subscribe to your channel.

6. Channel URL: If you have more than 100 subscribers, as a brand you might be eligible for a customized URL address. You also need to have a customized channel icon, channel art and for your account to be older than 30 days.

7. Channel links: In the About section of your channel, you should put the links to your business's website or other social media profiles. This makes it very easy for your audience to connect with you elsewhere.

Promoting on Other Social Media Platforms

YouTube is part of Google and if you do your SEO right, you will have no trouble ranking high in search engines. People will easily find your channel and videos whenever they are in need of your services or the product you have to offer. However, proper SEO will get you only so far.

To maximize your audience outreach you will have to do more, you will have to promote your channel and your videos on other social media platforms. This is yet another reason why you should opt for multiple platforms and establish your presence everywhere you think your targeted audience spends their time. Facebook, Twitter, Instagram, Pinterest, Linkedin, TikTok, are all relevant platforms marketers regularly use in order to reach the people and display their brands. You should not miss out. But this is why YouTube is so special! Other platforms will allow you to embed and post your YouTube videos. This way, they will reach not only the audience that uses YouTube's platform only, but also the people who are not using it and prefer to spend their time on Facebook, or on Twitter.

But you will have to introduce your YouTube videos to your audience on other social media platforms, in the right way. Even if you have already established a presence somewhere else, there is no such thing as a bad time to introduce YouTube videos to your audience. But you should refrain from bombarding your fanbase with YouTube commercials. Instead, introduce them gently, in a teasing way. Announce something new is brewing within your company. Make the introduction of a YouTube channel something special, something to anticipate. Once your channel gets published, create a special series that your audience will want to watch, and eagerly expect the next episode. Be sure your YouTube videos are of high-quality both technically and with their content. Don't forget to create a special hashtag that will come with your videos and organize a YouTube playlist to maximize the enjoyment of your followers.

Sharing is one of the best ways of cross-platform promotion. It is quite simple, but many businesses don't put enough effort into it. But this doesn't mean you should simply share your YouTube videos on other social media platforms. Of course, you would do that. But even more important and valued promotion is if other people and other companies share your content. You can always invite them to click share, but this is something professional, brand YouTube videos should avoid doing. Instead, opt for engaging your audience by replying to their comments. Don't simply say "Thank You" and move on. Try to start the conversation. Ask them to suggest something, or if they want to see something specific. The more attention you pay to your fans, the more likely they are to feel appreciated and they will engage in your videos. It is similar to other companies. Return the favor and share their videos on your social media platforms.

Another option for promoting your YouTube content on other social media platforms is to promote your channel as a whole, not just individual videos. You can embed your channel URL in the posts you dedicate to other social media such as Twitter, or Facebook. Intrigue your audience by saying they can discover more on the topic in your YouTube channel and they will click to check what you have to offer. In the same manner, you can cross-promote older videos. If you are touching on one topic on Facebook, but you made a YouTube video on the same topic some time ago, it is a great opportunity to post a link to that video on Facebook.

Chapter 13: YouTube Advertising

Advertising on YouTube is not the same as marketing on YouTube. However, it can be a part of the overall YouTube marketing strategy. Brands advertise on YouTube because they know this platform will ensure they reach a wide audience. But advertising on YouTube is a complex subject and if you take some extra time to learn about it, it will bring you great benefits. This chapter will teach you how to optimize your time and money and how to properly invest in YouTube advertising. You will also learn different types of ad formats, what options as a marketer you have, and what are video ad campaigns and how to set them up.

What You Should Know About Advertising

Advertising is using a very persuasive message to influence the clients and customers into buying a specific product or service. The goal of advertising is not only to increase sales but also to attract new customers. Therefore, the targeted market must be specifically defined. Only then a business can approach it with an effectively designed ad campaign. The first step in the advertising campaign is to establish the targeted market. This is the same as establishing your audience. You need to know who they are, and where do they come from, in order to effectively reach them. Once you establish the targeted market, you need to check the level of competition for the product or service you are offering. There is a chance you will have to compete for the audience with other companies who are offering the same or similar product/service.

Advertising takes as many forms as there are mediums. It can take the shape of online marketing, newspaper advertising, Yellow pages, TV or radio commercials, cold calling, or banner advertising. The type of advertising you chose will much depend on your targeted market. However, online advertising is steadily taking over as more and more people have access to the internet, and use it daily. This is why marketers simply cannot ignore online advertising. But no matter the type of advertising, your ads need to convey a certain message. To do the best job, ads need to be specifically designed to persuade an individual your business is their best choice. There are five main components of all ads that make up this design:

1. The headline: is the key attention-grabbing component of an ad. A simple, but effective headline needs to stir interest in the audience and make them want to learn more.

2. Subhead: is used only if a Headline needs clarification. It has the same role as the subtitles of the book.

3. Body copy: This is the main section in which the features and benefits of the product or service you are offering are highlighted.

4. Image: This is a visual aid that follows the ad. Its role is to help the audience visualize a product or a service.

5. Call-to-action: is the very end of the ad, in which you will invite your audience to do business with you.

When it comes to online advertising, there are several ways to do it. There is paid search advertising or pay-per-click (PPC). Advertisers will display their ads above organic search results, giving the paid ads the top spot on the search page. There is also social media advertising and you can use it to sponsor or boost your posts. Social media advertising will put your ad in front of the eyes of your targeted audience, and encourage them to engage. Sponsor content is another way of advertising online. Brands can subsidize blog posts or articles and through them, they can reference or recommend a product or a service. And finally, there are banners and display ads that are using the top of web pages as promotional space. They work similar to PPC, but instead of using mainly text, they focus on visual advertisement.

Paid Advertising on YouTube

YouTube allows marketers, companies, and businesses to post ads on its platform. This is a paid service, but there are various sets of rules YouTube implemented to make sure that by opting for this service, you get the most out of it. This is why businesses and marketers pay for an ad, only if a viewer watches it for at least 30 seconds. This way advertisers don't lose money and YouTube obliges itself to promote your ads to the targeted audience. In this deal, everyone's a winner. YouTube targets the audience to which it would play your ad based on their search history, both on the platform and on Google. But it also followers the viewing behaviors of the audience which helps YouTube decide who is the right target. But that doesn't mean you can't control your ads once they are out there. YouTube will allow you full control over your budget and paying method. You can set a limit and tell YouTube to stop displaying your ad once it hits a certain number of views, or once the budget you set in advance is all used up.

There are three main types of the paid advertisement on YouTube: TrueView Ads, Preroll, and Bumpers. Here is what each one of them entitles and how they work:

1. TrueView Ads: These ads are the standard of YouTube advertising. You will pay for this type of ad only if the viewer watches it or interacts with it (clicking on call-on-action). YouTube requires that TrueView ads must be between 12 seconds and 6 minutes long if they are skippable. There are two types of TrueView Ads: Video Discovery Ads (display in search results, or as video suggestions and related videos), and In-stream Ads (play before, during, or at the end of a video someone is watching)

2. Preroll Ads: These are non-skippable In-stream ads, and they can play before, during or after the main video. Preroll ads must be between 15 and 20 seconds long. Since these are shorter than the required 30 seconds of watch time, the unskippable ads use a different billing option known as CPM bidding (cost-per-thousand impressions).

3. Bumpers: These ads are the shortest type of YouTube ads. They last for six seconds and they always play before the chosen video. Since they are so short, advertisers need to be very creative about how to use this time and promote their business. Bumper ads also use the CPM bidding model of payment.

Launching a YouTube Ad Campaign

Once you have the video you want to use as an ad on YouTube, it's time to set up your ad campaign. Here is a step-by-step guide on how to do it. Keep in mind that the advertisement process on YouTube can be extensive and will require your time and dedication. It can also require some testing before you find the perfect strategy that will suit the needs of your business you are trying to promote.

Link YouTube channel with Google Adwords account. If you have multiple channels, repeat this process for each one of them. You will set up your advertising campaign using Google AdWords, but make sure the video is first uploaded to your YouTube channel. Once on the AdWords homepage, simply click on the "+Campaign" button. This will lead you to a new page where you will be able to choose the type of the campaign and set up its name. You should choose the "video" type from the drop-down menu. To ensure your video will be in TrueView format of the ad, select "In-stream or video discovery ads". Now you can set your budget, the amount of money spent per day.

Budget and Prices

There are various ways you can set up your budget and in order to do it properly, you need to understand some basic bidding strategies available to you. Most of the AdWords users use CPC (cost-per-click) bidding strategy. This is because people think the CPC strategy is less risky and easier to set up. But there is also an option to create CPV (cost-per-view) strategy.

1. Cost-per-click means that you will pay when users click on your ad campaign

2. Cost-per-view means you will pay for video views. This is the default setting in AdWords.

But YouTube will allow you to use only CPV bidding strategy. Although it would be nice to have options, CPV has a huge benefit. You will pay for the ad only if the viewer watched the first 30 seconds of it or the whole thing; or if he interacted with your ad. This means you are certain you are getting value for the money you are paying to YouTube. Once you set the bidding system, and you decide how much money you want to spend on the advertising, you are ready to go. But remember that you won't actually pay the price you set, at least not all the time. Here is how bidding works: if you set your price limit to be 0.20$ per view, but the next highest bid is only 15$, YouTube will charge you only 17$. The rule is one penny higher than the next highest bid.

Increasing your bid can help you get more traffic, but you need to keep in mind the money you are spending. You want to be comfortable with the price. Since the other advertisers are going to change their bid limits, the CPV system often fluctuates, and you need to keep track of it. AdWords will also allow you to set different bids for different target audiences. These are called customs bids and to set them up just click on the "Targets" tab under "All Video Campaigns", then click on "Bid". Now you should see a small icon that is labeled "Customize bids per format", click it and set bits for different targets.

Networks

AdWords will also let you decide where you want your ads to appear. You have two main options: YouTube Search or YouTube Videos. YouTube Search will display your ad on the search page, YouTube home page, channel pages, or as next to watch. YouTube videos will run your TrueView ad, and you can choose whether it will play at the beginning of the video, during it, or at the end. Most marketers opt for setting up different campaigns for YouTube Search and for YouTube Video ads. If you do it too, you will have better tracks of your ads' performance metrics.

Location, Language, and the Advanced

Settings

If you want to show your ad only in a particular location, the next step of setting your campaign will allow you to just that. You have given options to include all countries or to choose for yourself. The location tab will also let you see how many people you can reach at a particular location.

For more advanced targeting, AdWords will let you specify the operating system and the type of device your targets are using. This means you can set up your ad to ruin only for people who are using their mobile phones. You can even increase or decrease your bid if the ad is played on a certain device. You can also set up the language your audience is speaking.

Under the Advanced Settings section, you can set times and dates for the beginning and the end of your ad campaign. You can create a custom schedule, and limit the daily views for users. These settings are in place to help you get the most value for the money you are paying to run the ads.

Targeting and Advanced Targeting

Adwords will let you set up your targeted audience by age, gender, parental status, and by their interests such as cooking, music, lifestyle, movies, etc. You can always run different campaigns with different target audiences and see which will perform better. Advanced targeting will give you an option to target the individuals by keywords, topics, or websites. Keyword targeting is a powerful tool, especially when you are targeting individuals who answer to visual stimuli. Be sure to do your research, test some keywords and groups of keywords to see which will give you the best results, most clicks, and conversions.

Don't Forget to Check the Results

Once you run your ads, it is crucial to follow their performance. You can do this only by looking at the metrics and analyzing them. Impressions, engagement, views, and clicks, will tell you if your ad reached your targeted audience, and if they responded to it. Following the metrics is easy. Start with the Reporting Tab which you will find within Google AdWord. You will get tables, charts, and reports that are easy to read and understand. Reporting Tab will allow you to see the following:

Impressions: This represents the number of times your ad was shown to the viewers.

Views: This is the number of times someone watched your ad for at least 30 seconds. But this also counts the number of times someone interacted with your ad.

View rate: The rate is the percentage of the people who watched your ad when it was shown to them. To get the view rate, Google Ads uses a simple formula: total views divided by total impressions.

CPV: will tell you how much money you spent every time someone engages with your ad.

Earned actions: This section counts the subscriptions, likes, and additional views you earn after someone watches your ad.

Video viewership: This metric will show you how many people watched 25%, 50%, 75%, or 100% of your ad video.

Call-to-action overlays: The overlays are interactive elements on the video and are used to provide the viewers with more information.

They will drive the visits to your website, channel, or even other videos.

Remarketing lists: This will allow you to target the audience based on their previous interactions with your YouTube channel

Optimize Before You Launch a New One

After analyzing the metrics of your ads, you might come to a conclusion that your ads are not driving enough traffic to your website, or that there is simply not enough engagement of the viewers, you are not getting enough views. It is a perfect time to adjust some of the parameters and optimize your video campaign to perform better. Here are some tips on what you can do to give your ads a little bit of extra kick and drive the viewers to respond to them. By optimizing your ad campaigns, you will be able to reach new audiences, generate new clicks and conversions, and boost your search results.

Evaluate CPV

If you did everything you could to deliver a creative ad, able to capture the viewer's attention in the first five seconds, and if you did everything you could to find your targeted audience, but you are still seeing low views, it could be that you are being outbid, and it's time to adjust your CPV. If you find out you have to raise your CPV in order to reach a broader audience, it might mean two things: either your video is playing for several weeks and it reached creative exhaustion, or the competition is outbidding you. In both cases, raising your CPV bid would ensure that your video is played more often, to even more viewers and it could generate new conversions easily. However, if you find out that you can lower your CPV, it might mean that the competition is not strong at the given moment, and it is the right time to grasp the chance to gain more viewers and conversions.

Evaluate View Rate

View rate is the primary metric you should follow. It will tell you if your video ad is reaching enough people, and if they are interacting with it. In general, a video with a higher view rate will win more auctions, and it will pay lower bidding rates than a video that has low view rates. This is why you have to pay special attention to the targeting. It will ensure your video ad has more views than your competition, and that you would pay your ads at lower rates. You can do this by improving the creativity behind your ads. Shorter videos tend to have more views, minor tweaks such as adding captions, or improving the introduction can take you a long way. You might find out that you just adjusted your ad to reach a completely new audience of which you weren't even aware.

Evaluate CTR

This is an important measure if your goal is to use YouTube advertising to drive more traffic to your website. To achieve this, you should look into narrowing your targeted audience. Understanding what your viewers want and what they need is the first step in successfully picking the right demographic. If needed, adjust your audience's age, gender, parental status, interests, and affinities. But don't forget to evaluate the topics and keywords of your ads, as they play an important role in giving your audience just what they were searching for. If you want to exclude certain viewers, you can add topics and certain demographics to the exclusion list and your ad won't be played to them. This should be done only if the metrics show you that your ad has no response with a certain type of audience. By excluding them, you will ensure your video ads are played only to the people who find them relevant.

Section 5:
Aiming and Achieving
Your Long-Term Goals

Chapter 14:
Becoming an Influencer

Influencer, someone who wields influence, is an aspiration of many modern young people. But the term itself bears dual value. It is used for people who are business owners, and experts in their field, and celebrities, but it can also be used as an insult to render meaningless someone's social impact. While some elected officials are considered influencers, so are some well-dressed pets. The influencer culture so popular today is tightly close to consumerism and the rise of technology. An influencer is anyone who has the power to affect the buying habits of people. They would resort to uploading original content, often sponsored, that drives their followers to desire and to buy certain products or services. Influencers use various social media platforms and upload photos, videos, blog posts, reviews, or stories in order to change people's online behavior and influence their spending habits. Influencers have to be creative and authentic, and they have to wield a certain dose of authority in order to be able to affect their followers.

What it Means to Become an Influencer

Influencers are people who already established themselves as creators on YouTube, they grew a base of followers and are now able to monetize their videos by influencing their followers' buying behavior. Influencers get paid by the sponsors, for their promotion of a certain product or service. But because of what they do, influencers are often seen as something negative and often unwanted. Nevertheless, they manage to drive the market for their sponsors, for various brands and companies. Marketers need influencers and they need their approach to the audience. But How are influencers different from YouTube content creators? They also create their original videos and upload them for everyone to see, just like creators do. The difference is in self-expression. While influencers are used by marketers and companies to promote the business, creators are doing it for self-expression.

But whether the term "influencer" will have a negative or positive connotation largely depends on the age of the audience or YouTubers. Old people tend to sneer at the term, but young generations see it as a career title to which they should aspire. While millennials tend to call themselves "creators" even if they indulge in the job of influencers, zoomers intentionally call themselves influencers. They enjoy the title because it proves they are able to turn their social connections into an income. Younger generations are also aware that if they wear the title of an influencer as a badge of honor, they would attract brands willing to sponsor them. Brands themselves quickly adopted the term and even the marketing agencies started allocating money for "influencer marketing". But the truth is also those creators tend to work on YouTube only, while today's influencers have to be present on multiple social network platforms. Building their presence solely on YouTube means limiting themselves to one type of audience. Instagram and Facebook are becoming very popular options, especially since they also introduced the option of monetization through sponsorship deals.

YouTube Influencers in Every Field

Because YouTube is used by millions of people every hour, brands search for YouTube influencers with lots of subscribers, through which they would push their product. But not every channel with lots of subscribers is eligible to become influencers. The type of content one produces plays a key role. Here is a list of some of the biggest names out there who are recognized as the influencers to go to, in their respective niches.

1. Fashion, Lifestyle, and Beauty: This is a very broad category but this is because the lines between them are not very well defined. Make-up artists will often suggest interesting fashion combinations to wear and the fashion influencers often talk about their lifestyle and diet. Names worth mentioning in this category are Zoe Sugg and her fashion channel Zoella. She reaches 11.5 million subscribers all over the world and she offers beauty hacks, shopping sprees, make-up tutorials, etc. But the biggest name out there is Kids Diana Show, a lifestyle channel based in Ukraine that reaches astonishing 75.7 million subscribers. This channel is owned by a young girl Diana. She posts lifestyle-related videos targeting families and parents of young children.

2. Sports and Fitness: This is one of the most popular categories on YouTube and its popularity is still growing, mainly due to COVID19, lockdown, and people searching for new ways to stay fit during the hard times when they have to stay put. But the most popular channel in this category is actually integrating sports with comedy. Dude Perfect gathers 55.6 million subscribers.

3. Gaming: Another very big category is gaming. Since gaming became a mainstream culture, this category is not a small niche anymore. Its biggest star is definitely PewDiePie, with over 109 million subscribers. He is a Swedish YouTube star and aside from rocking the world of gaming, he is also the most subscribed individual creator on YouTube. The size of his subscribers and his charming personality make him one of the most wanted influencers.

4. Tech: Shoppers looking for tech products are the audience most likely to search for videos in order to decide on their choices. They also love to use YouTube to educate themselves about what is new out there! The name that stands out in this category

is certainly Marques Brownlee, and his channel is named after his initials MKBHD (HD stands for High Definition). He has 13.7 million subscribers and offers amazing tech review videos that are highly engaging.

5. Entertainment: Watchtime for entertainment videos is incredibly high. Since younger generations use YouTube instead of TV, it is no wonder they prefer to search for quick entertainment on this platform. One of the biggest influencers out there in this category is Toronto-based Lilly Singh with over 14.9 million subscribers. She is diverse and creates comedy sketches as well as music videos, and much more.

6. Travel: The videos in this category are popular because they discover new worlds for their viewers. They are inspirational, informative, educational and they make us dream of unseen places. Among the biggest names out there is Jack Harries who gathers 3.78 million subscribers on his channel. But if you like to combine food enjoyment with travel, check out Mark Wiens with 7.41 million subscribers, or the Best Ever

Food Review Show channel that has 6.6 million subscribers.

Your Checklist to Becoming an Influencer

Becoming a YouTube influencer is not an easy task. The area is highly competitive and challenging. Young people all over the world want to become influencers because it is a valid career option out there, it's relatively new and exciting, and it is highly engaging. But becoming an influencer is much more than just posting high-quality YouTube content and hoping that a brand would notice you and want to work with you. First, you must gather your followers base and that alone is a difficult task. But it is from your viewership base that you can monetize your YouTube channel. Although it is a hard task, it's not impossible. There are millions of examples of rising YouTube stars out there, and you can be one of them. All you have to do is dedicate to it, and invest time in your career as an influencer. Here is a short checklist you can follow to make sure your new career takes off in the right direction.

1. Think about your goals, and what you want to achieve. This is a step you can

start doing even before you launch your YouTube channel. By asking yourself what you are hoping to get out of becoming an influencer, you will decide what types of content you need to create, and you will be able to define the targeted audience for your channel.

2. Develop your channel's goals and content. Although as an influencer you will work with brands and sponsors, you need to become a brand yourself. Once you establish what image of yourself you want to present, you will come up with the content that will support and follow that branded image.

3. Be consistent. Post frequently, at least once a week, and stick to your schedule. You are a brand, and your audience will want to know ahead when to expect new content from you. By being consistent and frequent you will increase your chances to attract new viewers.

4. Be original. this is a hard one, there are so many YouTube channels, and you have the impression all the topics are covered. However, originality is not only in the content itself but also in the way

you present that content. Come up with something new, original, and fresh that will capture your audience and make them want to stay on your channel.

5. Build a wide social presence for your channel. Create social media pages on different platforms and gather followers there. Cross-post your content and direct your audience from one platform to another.

6. Invest in your own website. Custom web design needs to reflect your brand and what you are representing. The website will be used to drive traffic to your YouTube channel, and you can even include a little store within it and sell your own merchandise.

7. Invest in the right tools. Invest in high-quality recording gear, and in a computer that will help you create high-quality content.

becoming an influencer doesn't happen overnight. Patience, hard work, and genuine interest in what you are doing will bring you a long way. keep an open mind and accept suggestions from potential sponsors, even if you never did them before. You might surprise yourself and discover many new things you are good at.

The Things You Can Do as an Influencer

Influencers are very powerful people. They are able to change the behavior of their followers, even more than Hollywood celebrities. The younger generations admire and follow more influencers than regular celebrities. Some of the influencers also have much more subscribers than celebrities. But why is that? The answer is pretty simple. New generations are more easily awed by someone who is relatable, who is just like them. The influencer is a guy next door. He is not an unapproachable musician or a movie star. He is the same as us, same as the most of the population, and he is a friend. However, there is a line that an influencer can cross, become a YouTube star, and stop being an influencer. Too many subscribers, too much fame, and an influencer will become unapproachable, he will lose his power to convince people into changing their behavior. When this happens, he stops being an influencer. As long as people can identify with you, and you present yourself as a dude from the neighborhood, you hold the power.

Brands are aware of this phenomenon that more popular influencers are less able to turn their viewers into customers. This is why recently, companies and businesses started turning to those influencers that have a smaller following base, but more loyal and more tightly targeted. These influencers are known as micro-influencers. They create a smaller base of subscribers, of carefully chosen demographic that will, for sure, easily turn into customers. Brands want to reach out to these smaller audiences rather than trying to mold a brand face out of one macro influencer (the one with a large base of followers). Speaking to the niche audience on more specialized subjects ultimately brings better results. But this is also how influencers are becoming more like brand's PR agents, and not their advertising weapon, a face behind the logo.

Companies and brands are missing a lot if they are not investing in YouTube influencers. The influencers are capable of not only bringing sales but also raising the awareness of the brand. Through their work, the influencers will drive conversions, generate leads, and a high ROI because their audience trusts them. This is why influencers may be an even better option than paid ads. However, the combination of the two gives the best results. Influencers are here to stay, and their popularity is not waning at all. The newer generations are identifying so much with them, that their dream job is not to be an astronaut, or a ballerina anymore. They want to become YouTubers, Influencers, and YouTube stars.

But before starting a collaboration with an influencer, do your research on them, and see if they are a good fit for your brand. You as a company won't have much influence over the content of influencer's videos. You can't control what they will say, how they will behave or what they will decide to show. Take for example Disney who had to break off their collaboration with PewDiePie, due to accusations that he is an antisemite. You don't want an influencer to ruin your brand's good image with his or her's unacceptable behavior.

Chapter 15: Making Money on YouTube

Content creators are not paid by YouTube for the videos they produce. The videos are not monetized by default. To make money from YouTube you have to go to settings and turn the monetization on. Still, this doesn't mean YouTube will simply pay for your content. Instead, it will offer you two different options: become a YouTube Partner, or have your video played on YouTube Premium. People think that only content creators with millions of subscribers can earn money on YouTube, but this is not true. The earning potential of your channel is determined by the engagement of your audience, not by the number of views or subscribers. Unfortunately, engagement isn't the only thing that will secure your earnings. You also have to carefully choose the niche you will cater to and explore the channel's revenues. Subscriber count does matter, but not in the scope it is believed.

There are YouTubers out there who earn millions from what they do. However, if you look closer, all that money is not earned solely through their content creation. They all have their own merchandise they sell outside of YouTube. They use their channel to drive traffic to the stores where they sell their merch. They all started small, by defining their targeted audience clearly, and delivering high-quality content. As their subscriber base grew, they started expanding their business from YouTube and creating a brand from themselves.

Earning a Living Through YouTube

Let's put aside the merchandise business of many YouTubers and concentrate first on how much money is possible to earn from YouTube alone. The amount of money YouTube will pay per view depends on many factors. Some of them are: the number of views, clicks, the quality of ads played during the video, the video's length, etc. The sum can be anywhere between 0.01$ to 0.03$ per ad view. On average, a YouTuber earns 0.18$ per ad view. That means that per 1,000 views, a YouTuber can earn on average around 18$. However, getting to the point where you can monetize your videos is hard work, and the people who get into the business usually do it out of their own passion to be in front of the camera, and to communicate with the audience. YouTube doesn't pay for the number of subscribers. But subscribers are still a valuable source of revenue because they generate ad views. They are also the ones who engage with your videos, they comment, share, and like, making your video visible to others. The more views your video gets, the more likely you would get paid.

A video can get you around 5$ per 1,000 views. But this is not an amount set in stone. The number will depend on the accumulated views as well as how many ads are integrated in your video. But this also means that 1,000,000 views will bring you around 5,000$. If you are a moderate influencer, this is already a significant amount of money you can earn. Keep in mind these numbers are estimates, and how much money you will actually earn depends on many factors. However, earning money from YouTube is a fast-developing economy and more and more companies are willing to spend their money on YouTube marketing. This also raises the chances of a good earning for content creators.

The ad placements are not the only way you can earn money through YouTube. Here are some other options out there for a YouTuber to earn his salary:

1. Affiliate links: Essentially, when a YouTuber is reviewing or mentioning a product of his "favorite brand" we're talking about affiliate links. When a viewer clicks on the link to the product (usually found in the description of the video) and makes a purchase, the YouTuber will earn a commission.

2. Merchandise: We already mentioned that YouTube stars usually sell their own merchandise through their own shops, hosted outside of YouTube. The most common things YouTubers who made a brand out of their channel sell are accessories such as shirts, bags, hats, etc. But some also make toys or fashion products of their own.

3. Sponsorship: If your channel has a large number of subscribers, brands will approach you for a partnership. They will want to sponsor you in turn for product reviews that will increase their sales.

There are millions and millions of content creators on YouTube, and most of them don't earn anything. But the majority of people who manage to monetize their YouTube channels, earn a decent living. It is not much, but it can do well as a side hustle or even an average monthly salary. And in the end, there is a small and elite club of YouTubers who is able to make an extraordinary income, counted in millions of dollars per year. They are YouTube stars, and there are just over 2,000 of them. Many of these stars are already established musicians such as Rihanna, but many more are just ordinary people who managed to succeed. The hardest part of earning a living from YouTube is the very start, earning your first dollar. But if you offer quality content and grow your audience, it will become easier. Once you establish your name and brand, things will just start to develop on their own as the brands will seek to sponsor you and to work with you.

The YouTube Partner Program (YPP)

The YouTube Partner Program is one of the easiest ways to start earning money through YouTube. This program will allow the creators to monetize their content by allowing the ads to play during their videos. If you join YPP you will become a part of the revenue-sharing model which helps both creators and YouTube to stay in the business. This means that when you allow ads to be added to your videos, and your viewers watch them, you will share the revenue with YouTube taking 45% and giving you 55%. But to become a partner, your channel needs to become eligible. The minimum requirements to apply for the YPP are:

1. Have a minimum of 1,000 subscribers on your channel

2. Have at least 4,000 hours of watch time in the past 12 months

3. YPP is supported in the country where you reside

Once you reach these milestones, you will become eligible to apply for the YPP. And here is how you can do that. In the YouTube Studio click on "Monetization", and you will be brought to the YPP application page. There are three steps you need to fulfill in order to become YouTube Partner:

1. Read and agree to the YPP terms of service

2. Set up a Google AdSense account and connect it to your channel

3. Wait for YouTube to review your channel and approve your application.

YouTube's policy promises you that the decision regarding your application will be made in 30 days. However, most of the channels that joined YPP testify that it took YouTube only around 72 hours to respond. YouTube reviews applications even during the weekends. A significant number of applications get declined, but don't let that discourage you. If you are not accepted to the YPP on your first try, improve your channel to fit YouTube's policies and try again. YouTube will allow you to reapply in 30 days.

YPP will allow you access not only to revenues from ads but also some extra monetization features such as:

1. Super Chats & Stickers: These are monetary donations of viewers during live streams. To become eligible for the feature you must be at least 18 and live in a country where the feature is available.

2. Channel Membership: This is a paid membership to a channel where creators offer exclusive content to their viewers. To become eligible for this feature you must be at least 18 and have more than 30,000 subscribers.

3. Merch shelf: This is additional space below your videos where you can display

the merch you are selling. Again you must be at least 18 and have more than 10,000 subscribers.

4. YouTube Premium revenue: When someone who paid their monthly subscription to YouTube watches your video, you will get a percentage of that subscription.

Getting into YPP is only the first step in making money through YouTube, and it is worth it. If you create quality content that your viewers will like, you might even reach the status of a YouTube star!

Becoming an Affiliate

promoting a product in your YouTube videos and being paid for it is what affiliate marketing is. However, you can't just start doing it on your own. Putting links to the products you are reviewing in the video's description is not enough. First, you have to enter the affiliate marketing program with some of the businesses that offer it. There are many companies that want to do business with YouTubers, from Amazon to Microsoft, Loreal, or Maybelline. Once you sign up for their affiliate program, they will give you a unique URL that leads to their product, and that you can include in your video's description. This link will help the merchants keep track of the sales that came from your YouTube video. Each time a viewer clicks on a link in your video description, you will get paid. The brand you are working with might offer you a set price, or the percentage of the sale (the latter is more common). If you want to avoid applying to each brand, you can opt to work with affiliate marketing networks which will set you up with merchants willing to pay commissions. Clickfunnel and Affiliate are just some of these networks.

Affiliate marketing is a form of influencer marketing and it will require you to have a solid audience that enjoys your content and trusts you. keep in mind that items you are mentioning or reviewing to generate sales need to be in accordance with your youtube channel. If you are unboxing tech, and you gather an audience that is interested in tech, you don't want to sell them equipment for pets. You also want to affiliate only the products you actually trust. Don't ruin your image by reviewing and recommending a product that has low or no value to your audience.

If you wonder how and where you should include affiliate links, here is a quick guide that can help you:

1. The description of the video is the best place for the links, and you should always include them here. But sometimes, this is not enough as viewers might ignore the description. Make sure you encourage them to check the link out during your video. It can be as easy as saying "check out the link in the video description".

2. YouTube cards are in-video interactive boxes that let viewers click on them to find out more. These can be good places to put links as they are non-intrusive and subtle. They should be used only as an addition to the link in the video description.

Getting Sponsors

You don't have to have millions of followers in order to attract sponsors to your channel. Micro-influencers are prospering these days as the big brands came to realize that audiences are trusting them more than big YouTube stars. This is a good thing because it means you don't need to wait until your channel grows to extraordinary proportions in order to get sponsored. However, you do need to be patient. Nobody will sponsor a channel that is just starting. Sponsors make deals directly with content creators, without having the YouTube platform as a mediator. This means that YouTube will not push any requirements on your channel in order to get sponsorship. However, brands will have their own requirements because they cannot be associated with just anyone, same as you cannot. After all, your channel is your brand too. The trick is to find a good fit that will work both for your channel and for the sponsor.

There are three main things you should already be doing if you are a content creator looking into getting a sponsor.

1. Create quality content that is interesting, and that engages the viewers. Brands are always searching for high-quality content rather than the number of subscribers. You should also produce the content relevant to the brand that you are planning to work with.

2. Build your channel, and the brands will start searching for you. this doesn't necessarily mean you have to have lots of

subscribers. A quality targeted audience is much better for brands than a large pool of viewers of different demographics. Build a community and engage your audience. Make them trust you and feel comfortable on your channel.

3. Follow the rules. Both YouTube and various brands will not be interested in working with creators whose content is filled or associated with violence, abuse, sex; in general inappropriate content. If you break YouTube's rules and regulations your sponsors would abandon you, and you are at risk at getting banned from YouTube itself.

There are two types of sponsorship: paid sponsorship and product sponsorship. It is easy to conclude that paid sponsorship is when a brand directly pays a flat fee to the content creator for advertising. Product sponsorship is where the content creator is provided with a free product in exchange for its promotion. Many influencers start with product sponsorship and are satisfied to receive the item or service they are promoting. However, paid sponsorship is more lucrative, and worthwhile.

Don't rely on a sponsor to approach you. There are things you could do to ensure sponsorship even if you are a small channel with the possibility to grow. Some sponsors are even happy to help their influencers grow their followers base, and make them into the face of their brand.

Leave your email. be sure to put your contact information in the About section of your YouTube channel. This way, sponsors who are in search of new influencers will easily be able to find you. it might be a smart idea to create a separate, business email to which sponsors can reach you. This way, the sponsorship opportunities won't get buried among the spam mail.

Reach out. If you already have some specific brands in mind, and you are sure that you can produce content relevant to them, be the first to contact them. Go to their website and you will find the contact information of their marketing department. make your email unique, make it stand out from the crowd as some famous brands get many such offers from various influencers.

Use influencer marketing platforms. There are brands that are actively searching for influencers, and it could be a good idea to use platforms such as famebit.com or inzpire.me, to make yourself available. You would need to have at least 1,000 subscribers to sign up and connect your YouTube channel with your profile. These platforms will charge you, but only a percentage once you make a collaboration with a brand.

Selling Merchandise of Your Brand

Selling your own merchandise is the next step you should take, once you build your YouTube channel, and gain loyal subscribers. Your viewers love your content, they love what you do and they love you. They will want to support you, and they will want to own merch that is branded with your YouTube channel's name. This is very popular among the younger generations, just as people support their favorite bands by buying their t-shirts. Again, to successfully sell merch, you don't have to have millions of followers. As long as your subscribers are engaged, and love what you do, they will want to buy your products. You might get surprised by the fact that a YouTuber with 11,000 subscribers sells up to 6 pieces of merch every month. This means he is able to earn up to 70\$/month. Top YouTubers earn between 6 and 8 million dollars per year, just from selling their own merch. If you are a small channel, you won't get rich from selling the merch, but it is a lucrative side hustle. As your channel grows, so will the sales. Soon enough, you will be earning an exciting amount of money. you wouldn't want to miss that. And it is very simple for a YouTuber to start selling his merchandise. Here is how you do it!

Choose the design and type of your merch. Come up with an interesting logo, popular slogans, and visuals that your subscribers will love. You should also decide the overall presentation of these visuals. Should they be large and central, or smaller, repeating patterns or substantial empty space? At this point, you should also think about the products you want to sell. What are they, and how do they appeal to your audience. In fact, before launching your merchandise line engage your audience and ask them what they would like to see in your upcoming store. Depending on the demographics, your audience might have different needs and styles. Consider their gender, age, and interests.

Find where to sell your mech. There are print-on-demand businesses out there ready to produce the merch for you. However, you have to be careful and choose well. many of them use low-quality, unsafe and unethical products. Some of them offer limited designs too and you won't have enough room to create unique visuals for your merch. It is important to do the research and only then decide where you will produce and sell your merchandise.

Select your products. At this stage, you should already have a pretty good idea of what you want to sell. Phone cases, pillows, cups, and T-shirts, are always a safe bet. But you want to be unique and distinguish yourself from every other YouTuber who is selling his own merch. Most successful YouTubers try to sell merch that is relevant to their content. Think about selling a yoga mat if you are a fitness instructor, or if you are in a beauty niche, mirrors are a good option.

Finalize the design. Now that you know how your mercy is going to look like, you can decide where to put your logo, how the slogans will fit in the best, and think about the colors you want your merch to be. Think about taglines, sizes, different designs, patterns, etc. There are various online tools that can help you design your merch, and sometimes the producers will offer these tools on their websites too.

Promote your merch. YouTube will offer you a merch shelf and you can opt to display your merch directly on your YouTube channel, under your videos. But there is more you can do to drive traffic to your store. Add links to your merch in the video description section, or in the comments. Make a custom link for your channel's art or in YouTube cards. You can also share your store on other social media platforms such as Instagram and Facebook.

Getting Funds

Most YouTubers don't seek monetization of their channel because they want to get rich. Instead, they use it as means to earn a living. And while the majority is satisfied with collecting revenues through ads or through sponsorship, affiliations, and influencing, some resort to crowdfunding and donations. Crowdfunding is amazing because instead of bombarding your audience with ads, and throwing products at them, you will give them exactly what they want; the high-quality content created specifically for them. Mostly creative people and artists prefer crowdfunding, which is basically collecting smaller amounts of money from a variety of donors, instead of having one big patron.

There are many ways to crowdfund your YouTube channel:

1. Patreon: a website designed to serve the artists and creatives. Patreon is created in order to help artists on a monthly basis. This crowdfunding platform also offers you to reward your audience for their support with early access, or behind-the-scenes access, exclusive content, merch, live events, etc.

2. YouTube's own Sponsorship button. Recently, YouTube launched this service allowing people to make donations to their favorite content creators. In exchange, creators will reward their viewers with exclusive content.

3. Kickstarter: is a very popular crowdfunding site, but it is not limited to artists. Although some famous movie creators used this platform to fund themselves, the sight is more popular among the people who want to start their own production line or business. Kickstarter is also oriented towards

short-term projects, rather than supporting creators over a longer period of time.

4. Indiegogo: is amazing for small-scale production. Whether you are into music, movies, or games, there is a place for everyone who is into indie culture (it's even in the name of the website). People are attracted to fund the projects on Indiegogo because they believe in their success.

Licensing Your Content

Once a content creator uploads his video on YouTube, he can choose Licence options; Standard YouTube Licence, or Creative Commons. Here is what you need to know about the two, and the difference between them. Standard YouTube Licence, by which you grant the broadcasting rights to YouTube. This means that viewers can access your content only through YouTube and that they have no rights to reproduce or distribute your content. But they can share, because clicking the share button, or copying URLs to other social network platforms will lead new viewers directly to YouTube. Creative Commons means that other people can use parts of your content and use it to create their own production. Creative Commons allows other content creators to edit, change or alter your original video, but they cannot own the copyright to it and they have to clearly mention the original holder of the copyright. If you choose Standard YouTube Licence, other content creators who want to use your work must ask you for permission. You can accept or deny them the permission as you please. Even big media companies will have to ask for permission.

Conclusion

This book is meant for anyone who wants to start using YouTube for more than just browsing through videos. Whether you already own a YouTube channel, you are an established influencer, or just at the beginning of your journey, now you have the knowledge necessary to further to get started and grow. Making a video and uploading it on YouTube is easy. But that is not even half the work you should be doing in order to succeed. Even if you're an experienced videographer, you might hit some bumps along the road, and turn to this book for a solution or inspiration. Everybody needs help from time to time, and this book is designed in such a way that whether you read it from cover to cover, or intentionally target separate chapters, it will help you. Feel free to return to it whenever you feel insecure, when you need to refresh your knowledge, or if you need new ideas.

From how YouTube started, to making money on YouTube, the book tries to cover all the important topics out there. So many focus on nothing but the videography and marketing aspects when a YouTube channel is so much more than that. You learned why it is important to choose a niche, and how to build a channel that can satisfy the needs of your niche's audience. You also learned what equipment you might want to invest in in order to deliver high-quality content, how to manage and grow your channel and how to record, edit, and optimize your videos. Now that you know how SMM works, you can bring your company to the next level by producing some amazing YouTube commercials and ads. And finally, you learned how to monetize your videos, how to get paid for what you are doing, either through the YouTube Partnership program or on your own, through sponsorships and/or Kickstarter projects.

This book is a solution to all the YouTube troubles you might encounter in your new adventure of becoming a content creator. It's purpose is to serve you as a comprehensive instruction manual that touches on every topic related to YouTube instead of cherry picking the most obvious ones.

As promised, this book touches on the topics that cater to all possible YouTube users. Whether you want to use the platform for marketing, or you want to become the next PewDiePie, you now have the knowledge how to do it.

Finally, take another look at all the inspirational stories of successful Youtubers, examples of extraordinary channels, and all the lists of ideas on how to promote yourself, how to collaborate, and reach out to future sponsors. If anything, the goal of this book is to push you forward, and make you stop wondering "what if". Of course, there will be lots of "what if's" along the way, but now you have the knowledge of how to deal with them! So, take the next step and "just do it!". After all, if you enjoy it, if you are passionate about sharing your experiences with the audience, there is nothing that stands in your way, so go on! We want to hear your name called out as the next big YouTube star!

References

10 Things to Know About Copyright and YouTube. (2016, March 26). Dummies. https://www.dummies.com/business/marketi ng/social-media-marketing/10-things-to-know-about-copyright-and-youtube/

Advertising Definition - Entrepreneur Small Business Encyclopedia. (n.d.). Entrepreneur. https://www.entrepreneur.com/encyclopedia/ advertising

Anderson, M. (2020, December 24). *The 13 most popular types of videos on YouTube [Infographic].* IMPACT. https://www.impactplus.com/blog/most-popular-types-of-videos-on-youtube-infographic

Ang, C. (2020a, September 15). *Who's the Most Popular YouTuber in Every Country?* Visual Capitalist. https://www.visualcapitalist.com/worlds-most-popular-youtubers/

Ang, C. (2020b, September 15). *Who's the Most Popular YouTuber in Every Country?* Visual Capitalist.

https://www.visualcapitalist.com/worlds-most-popular-youtubers/

Asmelash, L. C. (2020, April 23). *The first ever YouTube video was uploaded 15 years ago.* CNN. https://edition.cnn.com/2020/04/23/tech/yo utube-first-video-jawed-karim-trnd/index.html

Attention Required! | Cloudflare. (n.d.). Canva. https://www.canva.com/create/youtube-thumbnails/

Baruah, B. P. (2015, September 22). *Why We Love YouTube (And You Should, Too!).* TO THE NEW   BLOG. https://www.tothenew.com/blog/why-we-love-youtube/

Benator, M. (2015, May 5). *Can You Still Become 'YouTube Famous'?* Vox. https://www.vox.com/2015/5/5/11562306/ca n-you-still-become-youtube-famous

Bond, C. (2021, January 23). *The Complete Guide to Getting Started With YouTube Live.* WordStream. https://www.wordstream.com/blog/ws/2020/ 04/27/youtube-live

Brand your channel. (n.d.). YouTube. https://creatoracademy.youtube.com/page/lesson/brand-identity

Brown, L. (2021a, March 1). *How to Optimize YouTube Tags/Title/Description for More Views.* Filmora. https://filmora.wondershare.com/youtube-video-editing/edit-youtube-video-title-description-tags.html

Brown, L. (2021b, March 1). *Standard YouTube License vs. Creative Commons.* Filmora. https://filmora.wondershare.com/youtube-video-editing/standard-youtube-license-vs-cc.html

Bullock, L., & Bullock, L. (2019, September 3). *How to Create High-Quality Video Content on a Budget.* Social Media Today. https://www.socialmediatoday.com/news/how-to-create-high-quality-video-content-on-a-budget/562098/

Collaboration. (n.d.). YouTube. https://creatoracademy.youtube.com/page/lesson/collaboration

Cox, S. (2018, February 22). *Essential YouTube Equipment For Starting Your Channel - What Do You Really Need?* Filmora.

https://filmora.wondershare.com/youtube/ess
ential-youtube-equipment.html

Create an account on YouTube - Computer - YouTube Help. (n.d.). Google. https://support.google.com/youtube/answer/1 61805

Davis, P. (2019, September 26). *How To Stand Out And Build A Remarkable Brand On YouTube » Endeavor Creative | Brand Strategy for.* Endeavor Creative | Brand Strategy for Service-Based Entrepreneurs. https://endeavorcreative.com/youtube-branding/

Determine Goals for Your YouTube Channel. (2016, March 26). Dummies. https://www.dummies.com/business/marketi ng/social-media-marketing/determine-goals-for-your-youtube-channel/

Dhawan, E. (2016, March 23). *How You Can Use YouTube to Turn Your Passion into a Career.* Forbes. https://www.forbes.com/sites/ericadhawan/2 014/12/17/how-you-can-use-youtube-to-turn-your-passion-into-a-career/#664b600f297c

Egan, K. (2020, December 24). *The difference between Facebook, Twitter, Linkedin,*

YouTube, & Pinterest [Updated for 2020]. Impact Plus. https://www.impactplus.com/blog/the-difference-between-facebook-twitter-linkedin-google-youtube-pinterest

Engage Your Audience - Creator Academy. (n.d.). Creator Academy. https://creatoracademy.youtube.com/page/course/fans

Everything Marketing Entails. (n.d.). Investopedia. https://www.investopedia.com/terms/m/marketing.asp

Find your niche. (n.d.). YouTube. https://creatoracademy.youtube.com/page/lesson/niche

Free - Add Music to Your Videos | Adobe Spark Video. (n.d.). Adobe Spark. https://spark.adobe.com/make/add-music-to-video/

From PewDiePie to Shane Dawson, these are the 23 most popular YouTube stars in the world. (2019, June 18). Business Insider Nederland. https://www.businessinsider.nl/most-popular-youtubers-with-most-subscribers-

2018-2-2/

Gardner, K. (2020, September 3). *Quality is in the eye of the beholder: new research on what viewers love.* Think with Google. https://www.thinkwithgoogle.com/marketing-strategies/video/video-production-quality/

Hardwick, J. (2020, March 25). *What are YouTube Tags and Which Ones Should You Add?* SEO Blog by Ahrefs. https://ahrefs.com/blog/youtube-tags/

Haughey, C. J. (2021, March 16). *17 Types of Video Content That People Actually Want to Watch.* Single Grain. https://www.singlegrain.com/video-marketing/10-useful-types-of-video-content-viewers-love/

Hook them with your channel trailer. (n.d.). Creator Academy. https://creatoracademy.youtube.com/page/lesson/trailers

Hosch, W. L. (n.d.). *YouTube | History, Founders, & Facts.* Encyclopedia Britannica. https://www.britannica.com/topic/YouTube

How to become a successful influencer, according to YouTube and Instagram stars.

(2019, September 5). *Business Insider Nederland.* https://www.businessinsider.nl/how-to-become-an-influencer-on-youtube-instagram?international=true&r=US

How to earn money on YouTube - AdSense Help. (n.d.). Google. https://support.google.com/adsense/answer/72857?hl=en

Justin Brown - Primal Video. (2018, August 1). *YouTube for Business! How to GROW Your Business with YouTube.* YouTube. https://www.youtube.com/watch?v=TQRTrJDn82w

Lang, M. (2020, December 24). *15 best video editing software and apps for any budget in 2020.* Impact Plus. https://www.impactplus.com/blog/video-editing-software

Lorenz, T. (2019, May 31). *The Real Difference Between Creators and Influencers.* The Atlantic. https://www.theatlantic.com/technology/archive/2019/05/how-creators-became-influencers/590725/

Lynch, M. (2020, September 26). *Smart*

Classroom Furniture for the 21st Century Students. The Tech Edvocate. https://www.thetechedvocate.org/youtube-valuable-educational-tool-not-just-cat-videos/

Martineau, P. (2019, December 4). *What's an Influencer? The Complete WIRED Guide.* Wired. https://www.wired.com/story/what-is-an-influencer/

Nazerali, S. (2020, September 3). *How YouTube influencers are rewriting the marketing rulebook.* Think with Google. https://www.thinkwithgoogle.com/marketing-strategies/video/youtube-influencer-marketing-rulebook/

Neil, S. (2017, November 29). *10 Oldest YouTubers in The World.* Oldest.Org. https://www.oldest.org/entertainment/youtubers/

Niazi, Z. (2020, May 18). *YouTube Ranking Factors – How to Rank Videos with YouTube SEO?* TimeZ Marketing. https://timezmarketing.com/youtube-ranking-factors

Oh, S. (2020, May 28). *YouTube SEO: How to Rank Your Videos From Start to Finish.* SEO Blog by Ahrefs.

https://ahrefs.com/blog/youtube-seo/

P. (2018, July 31). *The Challenges of Building a Successful YouTube Channel*. Pingler Blog. https://pingler.com/blog/the-challenges-of-building-a-successful-youtube-channel/

Patel, N. (2020a, January 23). *How to Optimize a YouTube Ad Campaign*. Neil Patel. https://neilpatel.com/blog/how-to-optimize-a-youtube-ad-campaign/

Patel, N. (2020b, September 3). *9 Ways to Improve Organic Reach and Beat the YouTube Algorithm*. Neil Patel. https://neilpatel.com/blog/youtube-algorithm-organic-reach/

Patel, N. (2020c, November 11). *How to Double Your YouTube Subscribers (Without Buying Them)*. Neil Patel. https://neilpatel.com/blog/the-real-secret-to-growing-your-youtube-subscribers/

Patel, N. (2021, February 12). *YouTube Marketing Guide*. Neil Patel. https://neilpatel.com/blog/youtube-marketing-guide/

Patton, D. (2020, April 28). *Avoid These 7 Common Video Editing Mistakes*. Welcome to

the TechSmith Blog.
https://www.techsmith.com/blog/common-video-editing-mistakes/

Price, A. (2018, January 15). *5 Tips for Creating Quality Video Content Even If You're Clueless How to Begin.* Entrepreneur. https://www.entrepreneur.com/article/30614 3

Reid, M. B. R. (2020, January 27). *How Video Editing Works.* HowStuffWorks. https://computer.howstuffworks.com/video-editing.htm

Renderforest LLC. (n.d.). *225 YouTube Video Ideas You Can Try Right Now.* https://www.renderforest.com/blog/first-youtube-video-ideas

S. (2019, December 9). *How to sell Merch on Youtube? 3 best strategies.* Sell Merch. https://sellmerch.org/welcome-back-to-my-channel-buy-my-merch/

Samuel, L. (2017, October 17). *YouTube Video Structure – What works!* Become A Blogger. https://iamlesliesamuel.com/25498/youtube-video-structure/

SEO Starter Guide: The Basics | Google Search

Central. (n.d.). Google Developers. https://developers.google.com/search/docs/beginner/seo-starter-guide

Shopify Encyclopedia. (n.d.). Shopify. https://www.shopify.com/encyclopedia/advertising

Silva, C. N. (2020a, February 24). *YouTube for Beginners: How to Set up Your Channel.* Search Engine Journal. https://www.searchenginejournal.com/youtube-beginners-set-up-channel/349814/

Silva, C. N. (2020b, February 24). *YouTube for Beginners: How to Set up Your Channel.* Search Engine Journal. https://www.searchenginejournal.com/youtube-beginners-set-up-channel/349814/

Smith, B. (2020, August 3). *YouTube Ads: Everything You Need to Know.* AdEspresso. https://adespresso.com/blog/youtube-ads-guide/

Soare, D. (2018, December 7). *How to Choose The Best Niche for Your YouTube Channel.* Medium. https://medium.com/@diana_21435/how-to-choose-the-best-niche-for-your-youtube-channel-2e0fb5f465b0

Soliciting Crowdfunding and Donations for Your YouTube Channel. (2016, March 26). Dummies. https://www.dummies.com/social-media/youtube/soliciting-crowdfunding-and-donations-for-your-youtube-channel/

Sorrentino, D. (2020, July 23). *A straightforward guide to making money with YouTube affiliate marketing.* Brafton. https://www.brafton.com/blog/video-marketing/youtube-affiliate-marketing/

Southern, M. (2020, June 29). *Google Explains How YouTube Search Works.* Search Engine Journal. https://www.searchenginejournal.com/google-explains-how-youtube-search-works/373189/

Sullivan, T. (2018, April 18). *A Beginner's Guide to Taking Great Video on Your Phone.* The New York Times. https://www.nytimes.com/2018/04/17/smarter-living/beginners-guide-phone-video.html

Sweatt, L. (2020, November 30). *YouTube Partner Program: How to Monetize Your Channel.* VidIQ. https://vidiq.com/blog/post/youtube-partner-program-guide/

Team, H. I. W. (2019, March 5). *How does*

YouTube work? How It Works. https://www.howitworksdaily.com/how-does-youtube-work/

The 5 YouTube Analytics Tools You Need. (n.d.). Brandwatch. https://www.brandwatch.com/blog/youtube-analytics-tools/

The Art of Improvement. (2018, November 11). *A Complete Guide to Goal Setting.* YouTube. https://www.youtube.com/watch?v=XpKvs-apvOs

The Latest YouTube Stats on Audience Demographics. (n.d.). Think with Google. https://www.thinkwithgoogle.com/data-collections/youtube-viewer-behavior-online-video-audience/

Top 10 Videography Tips. (n.d.). Desktop-Documentaries.Com. https://www.desktop-documentaries.com/videography-tips.html

Trounce, D. (2019, December 10). *7 Great Tools For Creating Your Own Video Tutorials.* Help Desk Geek. https://helpdeskgeek.com/free-tools-review/7-great-tools-for-creating-your-own-video-tutorials/

Types of Social Media Platforms & What's

Right for You. (2020, December 10). Titan Growth.
https://www.titangrowth.com/blog/types-of-social-media-platforms/

Video editing - Wikiversity. (n.d.). Wikiversity.
https://en.wikiversity.org/wiki/Video_editing

Wagner, A. (2017, August 23). *Are You Maximizing The Use Of Video In Your Content Marketing Strategy?* Forbes.
https://www.forbes.com/sites/forbesagencyco uncil/2017/05/15/are-you-maximizing-the-use-of-video-in-your-content-marketing-strategy/#23b2d5c93584

What Is Social Media Marketing? (n.d.). Investopedia.
https://www.investopedia.com/terms/s/social-media-marketing-smm.asp

wikiHow. (2021, January 13). *How to Upload a Video to YouTube.*
https://www.wikihow.com/Upload-a-Video-to-YouTube

Write smart descriptions. (n.d.). YouTube.
https://creatoracademy.youtube.com/page/les son/descriptions

YouTube Ads. (n.d.-a). *Beginner's Guide To*

Video Insights & Metrics —. YouTube Advertising.
https://www.youtube.com/intl/en-GB/ads/resources/beginners-guide-to-video-insights-metrics/

YouTube Ads. (n.d.-b). *Online Video Advertising Campaigns* —. YouTube Advertising. https://www.youtube.com/ads/

YouTube is 15 years old. Here's a timeline of how YouTube was founded, its rise to video behemoth, and its biggest controversies along way. (2020, May 30). Business Insider Nederland.
https://www.businessinsider.nl/history-of-youtube-in-photos-2015-10?international=true&r=US